MW00574549

Daily Skill Builders:
Spelling and Phonics
Grades 5–6

By
ANN FISHER

COPYRIGHT © 2007 Mark Twain Media, Inc.

ISBN 978-1-58037-407-1

Printing No. CD-404066

Mark Twain Media, Inc., Publishers
Distributed by Carson-Dellosa Publishing Company, Inc.

Table of Contents

Table of Contents (cont.)

Introduction to the Teacher

This edition of *Daily Skill Builders: Spelling and Phonics* is a powerful tool that will help you equip your fifth- and sixth-grade students with important phonics and spelling skills. Each half-page reproducible focuses on a specific skill, as shown in the Table of Contents. Correlated with state standards, these activities provide practice in essential tasks all upper elementary students need to succeed in language arts, in standardized testing, and, most importantly, in real life.

Both the No Child Left Behind Act and standardized testing require students to meet certain proficiency standards. The *Daily Skill Builders* in this book have been written with both of these sets of requirements in mind. (See the following website for National ELA Standards as supported by NCTE and IRA <http://www.ncte.org/about/over/standards/110846.htm>). Standards matrixes for selected states are provided on pages vi–viii. These give teachers the specific reading, writing, and language standards that are covered by each activity in this book.

The first portion of this book progresses logically through consonant blends and digraphs, short and long vowel sounds, vowel digraphs, and more. Students are given practice in reading, writing, and spelling frequently encountered at this grade level. As you already know, good spelling skills are often built on a solid foundation in phonics. Words are generally used in context so that students will know how to use the words they are learning.

On pages 17–27, you will find some especially helpful exercises that cover commonly misspelled and misused words. Many of the activities throughout the book ask students to read words, find them in a puzzle or unscramble them, place them in a sentence, and write them again. Practice, practice, practice!

Drills do not have to be boring, however. A wide variety of exercises are included in this book. The ever-popular word search puzzle is just one example of a fun format for students. While students are eagerly looking for words on a list, they are also rechecking the spelling of each word on their list. Often students will find the word in the puzzle, circle it, and write it. Crossword puzzles, scrambled words, context clues, and other formats are also used throughout this book.

In each section, activities are arranged from simplest to most difficult. Challenge your most advanced spellers with the word lists on pages 74–76. How many of these words do your students already know? How many can they learn by the end of the year?

Please note that most skills overlap among multiple sections of the book. For example, you can find practice with the tricky trio of *there-their-they're* on page 29 in the homophones section. The same words are highlighted again in many of the exercises where students are asked to edit to correct errors in spelling and usage.

A comprehensive answer key appears in the back of the book, making this resource one that is very simple to use.

Look through all the pages of this book when you begin to use it. Pay attention to pages with special activities you know you will want to cover. Make notes in the margins or on sticky notes attached inside the cover to get the most mileage out of these *Daily Skill Builders: Spelling and Phonics*!

How to Use This Book

Photocopy the pages that contain the activities you want to use. Cut the activities apart and assign one at a time. These exercises have been designed primarily for your students to complete independently. These will support and enhance your spelling and language arts curriculum, and can be used sequentially.

Additionally, the exercises can be used:
- as daily warm-ups;
- as seatwork while other students are in reading groups;
- as a diagnostic tool. Since the exercises are very short, you can ask students to complete them *before* you begin a new unit so that you'll know how much time students may need to spend on each skill;
- as a review before testing. Give all of your students, or just the ones who need it most, a quick brush-up on weak areas prior to testing;
- for partner work. Assign pairs to complete a drill together;
- to supplement centers in your room on similar topics;
- as bridge-builders with parents. Send home just one activity at a time and ask students to complete the page with a family helper. This is a simple way to involve parents in key skill-building activities.

In short, use these *Daily Skill Builders* any and every way you can to make the most of all the tools packed inside. Expect your students' reading, writing, and spelling skills to grow throughout the year!

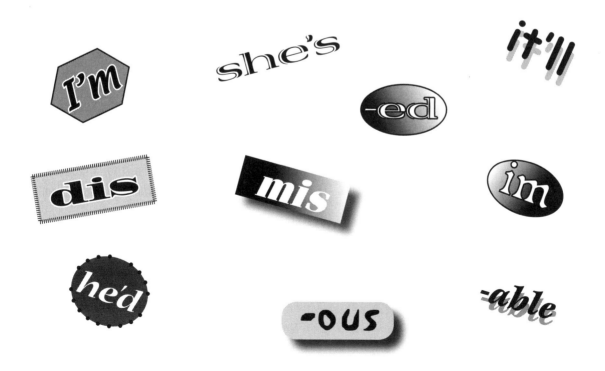

California Standards Matrix for Grades 5–6

LANGUAGE ARTS STANDARDS	ACTIVITIES
READING	
Understand and explain frequently used synonyms, antonyms, homographs, and homophones.	55, 56, 57, 58, 59, 60, 61, 62, 63, 64, 65, 66, 67, 68, 69, 70
Use word, sentence, and paragraph clues to determine meaning of unknown words.	1, 4, 6, 7, 9, 11, 12, 13, 15, 16, 17, 18, 20, 21, 22, 23, 26, 27, 28, 37, 38, 39, 41, 42, 43, 44, 46, 47, 48, 49, 50, 75, 76, 77, 78, 79, 80, 81, 82, 83, 84, 89, 90, 94, 95, 96, 97, 99, 100, 101, 102, 103, 104, 105, 106, 107, 112, 114, 115, 118, 120, 124, 130, 131, 132, 135, 153, 155, 156
WRITING	
Create well-developed, multiple-paragraph narrative and expository compositions.	3, 58, 116
Use a variety of organizational patterns, including comparison and contrast; organization by categories; and arrangement by spatial order, order of importance, or climactic order.	14, 29, 100, 133, 134, 137, 147, 150, 151, 157, 158, 159, 160, 161, 162, 163, 164
LANGUAGE CONVENTIONS	
Use simple, compound, and compound-complex sentences; use effective coordination and subordination of ideas to express complete thoughts.	1, 3, 8, 13, 14, 15, 22, 30, 40, 45, 58, 62, 64, 93, 116, 117, 148, 149, 152
Identify and properly use indefinite pronouns and present perfect, past perfect, and future perfect verb tenses; ensure that verbs agree with compound subjects.	111, 121, 122, 124
Use correct capitalization.	125, 126, 127, 128, 129, 130, 131, 132, 133, 134, 136, 141, 142, 143, 154, 156
Spell roots, affixes, contractions, and syllable constructions correctly.	1, 4, 8, 10, 13, 14, 16, 17, 21, 22, 24, 26, 31, 32, 33, 34, 35, 36, 40, 45, 46, 51, 52, 53, 54, 58, 71, 72, 73, 74, 83, 85, 86, 89, 91, 92, 93, 98, 108, 109, 110, 111, 112, 113, 114, 116, 117, 119, 120, 121, 122, 123, 133, 134, 136, 138, 139, 140, 143, 144, 147, 148, 149, 150, 151, 152, 153, 154, 155, 156

Florida Standards Matrix for Grades 5–6

LANGUAGE ARTS STANDARDS	ACTIVITIES
READING	
Study word parts and meanings consistently across curricular content (e.g., affixes, multiple meaning words, antonyms, synonyms, root words, homonyms, homophones).	7, 10, 13, 17, 19, 21, 24, 25, 44, 51, 55, 56, 57, 58, 59, 60, 61, 62, 63, 64, 65, 66, 67, 68, 69, 70, 71, 72, 73, 74, 75, 76, 77, 78, 79, 80, 81, 82, 83, 84, 85, 86, 87, 88, 90, 91, 92, 93, 94, 95, 96, 97, 99, 100, 102, 103, 105, 106, 107, 108, 111, 112, 135, 138, 139, 140, 144
Use resources (e.g., dictionary, thesaurus, encyclopedia, Web sites) to clarify word meanings.	1, 5, 16, 64, 76, 85, 87, 92, 97, 107, 113, 162
Use a variety of strategies to monitor texts (e.g., rereading, self-correcting, summarizing, checking other sources, using context and word structure clues).	1, 2, 4, 6, 9, 11, 12, 15, 16, 18, 20, 22, 23, 26, 27, 28, 37, 38, 39, 41, 42, 43, 46, 47, 48, 49, 50, 52, 53, 54, 69, 70, 89, 90, 98, 101, 104, 114, 118, 121, 122, 124, 129, 130, 131, 132, 153, 154, 155, 156
WRITING	
Use an effective organizational pattern and substantial support to achieve completeness.	14, 18, 116
Use a variety of sentence structures to reinforce ideas.	1, 3, 8, 14, 15, 22, 29, 30, 40, 45, 58, 93, 116, 148, 149, 152
Use conventions of punctuation and capitalization.	3, 8, 13, 14, 15, 22, 23, 24, 29, 30, 45, 58, 62, 64, 71, 74, 93, 116, 125, 126, 127, 128, 129, 130, 131, 132, 133, 134, 136, 141, 142, 143, 144, 145, 146, 148, 152, 156
Logically sequence information using alphabetical, chronological, and numerical systems.	133, 134, 137, 147, 149, 150, 151, 157, 158, 159, 160, 161, 162, 163, 164
Use various parts of speech correctly in writing (e.g., subject-verb agreement, noun and verb forms, objective and subjective case pronouns, correct form of adjectives and adverbs).	3, 8, 13, 14, 15, 22, 29, 30, 45, 58, 62, 64, 93, 109, 110, 111, 113, 114, 115, 116, 117, 118, 119, 120, 123, 148, 152
Write for a variety of occasions, audiences, and purposes (e.g., letters to invite or thank, stories or poems to entertain, information to record, notes and summaries reflecting comprehension).	1, 3, 8, 13, 14, 15, 18, 22, 29, 30, 33, 34, 35, 36, 40, 45, 58, 64, 93, 116, 148, 152

Texas Standards Matrix For Grades 5–6

LANGUAGE ARTS STANDARDS	ACTIVITIES
READING	
Apply knowledge of letter-sound correspondences, structural analysis, and context to recognize words and identify root words with affixes.	1, 4, 6, 7, 9, 12, 13, 15, 16, 17, 18, 19, 20, 21, 24, 25, 27, 28, 44, 55, 57, 59, 60, 61, 62, 63, 65, 66, 67, 68, 71, 72, 73, 75, 76, 77, 78, 79, 80, 81, 82, 83, 84, 86, 87, 88, 89, 90, 91, 93, 94, 95, 96, 97, 99, 100, 101, 102, 103, 104, 105, 106, 107, 108, 128, 135
Locate the meanings, pronunciations, and derivations of unfamiliar words using a dictionary, a thesaurus, a glossary, and available technology.	1, 5, 16, 64, 76, 85, 87, 92, 97, 107, 113, 162
Follow strategies for comprehension while reading, such as rereading, using reference aids, searching for clues, and asking questions.	2, 10, 11, 16, 18, 20, 22, 23, 26, 37, 38, 39, 41, 42, 43, 46, 47, 48, 49, 50, 51, 52, 53, 54, 56, 69, 70, 74, 89, 90, 98, 103, 114, 118, 120, 122, 124, 129, 130, 131, 132, 137, 146, 150, 154, 156
WRITING	
Write for a variety of audiences and purposes, such as to express, to influence, to inform, to entertain, to record, to problem solve, and to reflect.	1, 3, 8, 14, 18, 40, 116, 148, 149, 152
Compose original texts, applying the conventions of written language, such as capitalization, punctuation, and penmanship to communicate clearly.	1, 3, 8, 13, 14, 15, 22, 23, 24, 29, 30, 125, 126, 127, 141, 142, 143, 144, 145, 146, 148, 149, 152, 154, 156
Write with accurate spelling of roots, inflections, affixes, and syllable constructions.	1, 3, 8, 13, 14, 15, 16, 22, 24, 29, 30, 31, 32, 33, 34, 35, 36, 40, 51, 52, 53, 54, 58, 62, 64, 69, 70, 85, 92, 94, 98, 116, 132, 133, 134, 135, 136, 137, 138, 139, 140, 141, 142, 143, 144, 145, 147, 148, 149, 150, 151, 152, 153, 154, 155, 156, 157, 158, 159, 160, 161, 162, 163, 164,
Use regular and irregular plurals correctly and adjust verbs for agreement.	109, 110, 111, 112, 113, 114, 115, 116, 117, 118, 119, 120, 121, 122, 123, 124
Write in complete sentences, varying the types, such as compound and complex, to match meanings and purposes.	1, 3, 8, 13, 14, 15, 22, 23, 24, 29, 30, 40, 45, 58, 62, 64, 91, 116, 148, 149, 152

ACTIVITY 1 Spelling With "S" Clusters: "scr" and "shr"

Name: _____

Date: _____

Finish spelling the *scr* or *shr* word in each sentence.

1. The restaurant offered a fabulous shr__ __ __ dinner for only $6.00.

2. Don't scr__ __ __ __ the rash because you will only make it worse.

3. The lifeguard heard shr__ __ __s and scr__ __ __s coming from the pool.

4. Dad always shr__ __ s important documents before he puts them in the trash.

5. Oh no! My favorite blue jeans have shr__ __ __ so much that they no longer fit!

6. When I don't know the answer to a question, I just shr__ __ my shoulders.

7. She scr__ __ __ __ her knee when she fell off her bike.

Think of two more *scr* words and two more *shr* words. (Or find words in the dictionary.) Write sentences using the words on your own paper.

ACTIVITY 2 Spelling With "S" Clusters: "squ" and "str"

Name: _____

Date: _____

How do you know when there's an elephant under your bed? To find the answer, follow these directions.

1. Find boxes with letters that can go here: str_____. Put an "X" in the boxes.
    Write the words that you can make: _____.
2. Find boxes with letters that can go here: squ_____. Put an "O" in the boxes.
    Write the words that you can make: _____.

Note: Some letters can be used with both *str* and *squ*.

ike	id	when	eet	irm	your	eeze
ong	nose	int	is	ing	ipe	squashed
again	aight	the	ange	are	ceil	eak

3. Write the words from the unused boxes in order from top to bottom and left to right:

    __ __ __ __ __ __ __ __ __ __ __ __ __ __ __ __ __ __ __ __ __ __
    __ __ __ __ __st __ __ __ __ __ __ __ing!

ACTIVITY 3 Spelling With "S" Clusters: Name:_____

"sc" and "sk"
Date:_____

Here's an interesting story that uses a lot of *sc* and *sk* words:

    A Boy Scout named Scott spotted a baby skunk. Scott scowled. He was scared that the skunk might spray him. But then Scott noticed that the skunk looked skinny and lonely. He became concerned that the skunk's mother was missing. So…

1. On the back of this page, finish the story. Use at least three more *sc* or *sk* words. You may use words from the word box, or other words of your own.

2. Circle the letter that comes next after *sc* or *sk* for each word in the word box.
   What letters follow *sc*? _____
   What letters follow *sk*? _____

scar	score
skunk	scare
skirt	skinny
scout	skate
skid	scale
scooter	skip
skirt	scatter
scold	scale
sky	scowl

ACTIVITY 4 Spelling With "S" Clusters: Name:_____

"sc" and "sch"
Date:_____

The pronunciations are given for 12 words that begin with *sc* or *sch*. Write the correct *sc* or *sch* spelling for each word. Example: sĕnt = scent

1. sko͞ol _____

2. sĭz′ ərz _____

3. skēm _____

4. sī′ əns _____

5. sko͞o′ ner _____

6. sēn _____

7. sī′ ən tĭst _____

8. skŏl′ ər _____

9. sē′ nə rē _____

10. sĕp′ tər _____

On another piece of paper, write a sentence for three of these words.

G. WASHINGTON SCHOOL

ACTIVITY 5 Spelling With Consonant Digraphs: "ph"

Name:_____

Date:_____

Write each *ph* word in the correct category. Some words may be used more than once. Use a dictionary if you need help to learn the meaning of a word.

pheasant	phlox	phonics	physician	alphabet
phoebe	nephew	hyphen	elephant	pharmacist

A. Living things

B. Things to help you read and write

C. People

_____

_____

_____

_____

_____

_____

On your own paper, write each *ph* word again.

ACTIVITY 6 Spelling With Consonant Digraphs: "wr"

Name:_____

Date:_____

Think of a word that begins with *wr* for each definition below. Write each word in the blanks.

1. a tool with jaws, used to grip and turn things like bolts and nuts   wr __ __ __ __

2. to twist and squeeze to force water out   wr __ __ __

3. the joint where the hand and arm come together   wr __ __ __

4. opponents who try to grab or throw each other to the ground   wr __ __ __ __ __ __ s

5. to ruin or destroy   wr __ __ __

6. very great anger   wr __ __ __

7. a paper or other material that is used to cover something   wr __ __ __ __ __

8. a small crease or fold on a smooth surface, like skin or cloth   wr__ __ __ __ __

On your own paper, write your own definitions for these *wr* words:

wreath   wriggle   wrong   wry

ACTIVITY 7 Spelling With Consonant Digraphs: "ti"

Name: _____

Date: _____

Sometimes the *ti* makes the *ch* sound, as in *question*. Other times, the *ti* makes the *sh* sound, as in *direction*. Write a *ti* word for each clue in the crossword puzzle.

1. opposite of answer
2. to speak of briefly
3. If you want to learn, please pay _____!
4. idea for others to consider
5. absolutely necessary
6. capable of developing
7. extreme fatigue
8. The lightbulb was perhaps Edison's greatest _____.

ACTIVITY 8 Spelling With Consonant Digraphs: "ti"

Name: _____

Date: _____

"In your condition, you should not sit in that position," said the doctor to the patient.

Can you make five sentences with at least three *ti* words in each? Choose words in which the *ti* spells the *ch* or *sh* sound. You may use words from the word box or find some of your own.

addiction	action
direction	motion
station	section
connection	correction
selection	ration
providential	lotion
presidential	election
detection	fraction
locomotion	notion
protection	reduction

1. _____
2. _____
3. _____
4. _____
5. _____

Use another sheet of paper if you need more room.

ACTIVITY 9   Spelling Words With the Short "a" and Short "e" Sound

Name: _____

Date: _____

Supply a word that makes sense in each blank. Write a word that contains the vowel sound given at the end of each line. More than one word may work for some blanks.

1. Was the news report based on _____ or opinions?   (ă)

2. The _____ of string was not enough to tie the balloon to the tree. (ĕ)

3. Whoever _____ the closest number wins the prize!   (ĕ)

4. I'm hoping my _____ can visit us soon. (ă)

5. It takes extra _____ to grow _____ during a drought.   (ĕ)

6. Mr. Rancher's _____ have always had enough _____ for grazing.   (ă)

7. How much money did Julia _____ on her new camping _____?   (ĕ)

ACTIVITY 10   Using the Short "e" Sound, Spelled "ea"

Name: _____

Date: _____

Follow the directions in each line.

1. Write at least three *ea* words that rhyme with *head:* _____

2. Write three words that end in *-easure:* _____

3. Write three *ea* words that rhyme with *heather:* _____

4. Circle the words with a short *e* sound: breath   wreath   death   breathe   wheat

5. Circle the words that can rhyme with *bed:*   lead   bead   read   feed   said

6. Write a sentence that uses *meant:* _____
   _____

7. Write a sentence that uses *instead:* _____
   _____

8. Write a sentence that uses *deaf:* _____
   _____

ACTIVITY 11   Spelling Words With the Short "i" Sound

Name: _____

Date: _____

Circle each *i* that spells the short *i* sound in the words in the box. Then write the correct word in each blank.

1. The hospital patient was allowed only one _____.
2. When will you be _____ your bowl of popcorn?
3. It helps to know how to alphabetize when you use a _____.
4. The _____ speed on the highway is 45 m.p.h.
5. If you can't find an item in our store, please _____ at the customer service desk.
6. In the summer, it's often cooler _____ than outside.
7. The _____ table we built out of old boards was not very sturdy.

> inside
> primitive
> inquire
> dictionary
> visitor
> finishing
> minimum

ACTIVITY 12   Spelling Words With the Short "i" Sound With "y"

Name: _____

Date: _____

Find a word in the puzzle for each definition. Each word contains a *y* that makes the short *i* sound, as in *gym*. Write the words you find in the blanks.

1. a legend _____
2. the beat of a song _____
3. stands for something else _____
4. large round metal instruments that are hit or crashed together _____
5. a make-believe fairy _____
6. music for an orchestra _____
7. one way to do things _____
8. part of a word _____
9. tube _____
10. related to the body _____
11. something unknown _____
12. to feel sorry for someone _____
13. a word that has the same meaning as another _____

J	L	S	N	L	O	B	M	Y	S
X	A	M	Y	R	H	Y	T	H	M
M	C	E	M	M	Z	B	C	O	Y
Y	I	T	P	L	P	Y	W	C	S
N	S	S	H	O	L	A	Y	E	T
O	Y	Y	J	I	P	M	T	H	E
N	H	S	N	Y	B	O	G	H	R
Y	P	D	G	A	H	T	Y	M	Y
S	E	E	L	B	A	L	L	Y	S
R	O	S	Y	M	P	H	O	N	Y

Bonus: Can you find this tricky three-letter word? to cheat or swindle someone

ACTIVITY 13 Spelling Words With the Short "o" Sound

Name: _____

Date: _____

Many two-syllable words with double letters contain the short *o* sound, such as *bottle*. Can you figure out which consonants are missing in each of these words? Add the missing double letters to each of these words. Some have more than one answer.

1. fo _ _ ow
2. co _ _ on
3. do _ _ ar
4. go _ _ le
5. ro _ _ er
6. bro _ _ oli
7. wa _ _ le
8. go _ _ ip
9. no _ _ le
10. sho _ _ er
11. swa _ _ ow
12. thro _ _ le

Now use three of these words in sentences.

1. _____

2. _____

3. _____

ACTIVITY 14 Spelling the Short "u" Sound

Name: _____

Date: _____

Build a sentence pyramid. Use as many words with the short *u* sound as possible. Here is an example.

Sentence with one word:	Run!
Sentence with two words:	Run, Uncle!
Three words:	Suddenly, Uncle runs.
Four words:	Suddenly, Uncle must run.
Five words:	Suddenly, Uncle runs and fumbles.
Six words:	Suddenly, Uncle runs, fumbles, and mumbles.

(Only two words in six sentences are not short *u* words.)

Now build a sentence pyramid on your own paper. Underline every short *u* word that you use.

    7

ACTIVITY 15 Using Words With
"Vowel-Consonant-Silent 'e'" Pattern

Name: _____

Date: _____

Circle the right word at the end of each line.

1. Which is a sum of money you might have to pay as a penalty?   fin   fine

2. Which is an idea of how to do something?   plan   plane

3. Which is a topic for a paper?   them   theme

4. Which is the past tense of *ride*?   rod   rode

5. Which means to give up?   quit   quite

On another piece of paper, write your own questions for these pairs of words. Use a dictionary if necessary.

hug/huge   din/dine   rid/ride   rat/rate   ton/tone

ACTIVITY 16 Spelling Words With
the Long "a" Sound

Name: _____

Date: _____

The long *a* sound can be spelled in many ways, as you can see in these words:
apron   made   maid   stay   neighbor

Follow these three directions:
*   Circle all the misspelled words you find.
*   Rewrite each misspelled word correctly on your own paper.
*   In the first paragraph, underline all syllables with the long *a* sound.

The plan for the Robins to win the baseball gaim was plane to everyone. The way to make the Eagles strike out was for the Robins to wave their arms, race around the dugout, and scream loudly enough to give every Eagle player a headake.

It was now the eith inning and time to work the plan. The score was tied. The coach was afrade his teme might not pull through.

"I ame to win this game!" Coach yelled. "Let's claym victory! Let's shaip up! Let's wave our arms and scream!" The coach had already straned his voice enough. "No complaning, team. Just pay close attention. Hit. Run. Throw. Catch. And make the other team strike out. It's very simple."

The pep talk payed off. The Robins struck out all the batters in the eigth and ninth innings. And the last Robins batter hit a home run way out of the park!

8

ACTIVITY 17 Spelling Words With the
Long "e" Sound

Name:_____

Date:_____

If something is simple, that means it is easy. Can you think of a synonym for these words that contains the long *e* sound? Write your answer(s) in the blanks.

1. a plan   _____

2. finished   _____

3. sickness   _____

4. often   _____

5. right away   _____

6. algae   _____

7. search for   _____

8. striped animal _____

9. depart   _____

10. defeat   _____

Now put a star by each number in which both the clue and the answer have the long *e* sound. Can you write any more pairs like these?

_____

_____

ACTIVITY 18 Spelling Words With the
Long "i" Sound

Name:_____

Date:_____

Change one letter of the original word at a time to make a new word that matches each definition. Many of your words will contain the long *i* sound.

1.   guy   2.   dial

opposite of sell   ___ ___ ___   kind of pickle   ___ ___ ___ ___
young male   ___ ___ ___   medicine tablet   ___ ___ ___ ___
kind of bean   ___ ___ ___   heap   ___ ___ ___ ___
clever   ___ ___ ___   5,280 feet   ___ ___ ___ ___
to move with wings ___ ___ ___   gentle   ___ ___ ___ ___
cook in oil   ___ ___ ___   brain   ___ ___ ___ ___
not wet   ___ ___ ___   to look for and discover ___ ___ ___ ___
attempt   ___ ___ ___   excellent   ___ ___ ___ ___
weep   ___ ___ ___   to eat dinner   ___ ___ ___ ___

Now put a * after each long *i* word.

Try to make your own change-a-letter puzzle. Start with one of these long *i* words:
        why   pie   life   wide

ACTIVITY 19 Spelling Words With the
Long "o" Sound

Name: _____

Date: _____

These words have been divided into syllables. Draw a line over the *o* in each word with the long vowel sound.

mo ment	ra di o	en roll	bro ken
cloth ing	o cean	post age	lo cal
toast er	ho tel	gold en	host ess

Now write these words again, without dividing them. Write them in the correct column to show which type of syllable has the long *o* sound. Two are done for you.

Open Syllable
moment

_____

_____

_____

_____

_____

Closed Syllable
enroll

_____

_____

_____

_____

_____

ACTIVITY 20 Spelling Words With the
Long "u" Sound

Name: _____

Date: _____

Add the missing consonants to spell words that make sense in each sentence. Each word will have the long *u* sound.

1. On the Fourth of July, we always have a big __ a __ __ e __ ue.

2. It's nice when children are able to a __ u __ e themselves for awhile.

3. The diver performed a daring __ e __ __ ue.

4. Don't you wish you could see into the __ u __ u __ e?

5. A good sense of __ u __ o __ will get you through difficult times.

6. It is our u __ ua __ policy to require a note from home after an absence.

7. The new __ __ a __ ue in the city park is __ u __ e!

8. The police decided to __ u __ __ ue the suspect over state boundary lines.

b b
c c
f
g
h h
l
m m
p
r r r r r
s s s s s
t t t

ACTIVITY 21   Recognizing Similar Vowel Sounds

Name:_____

Date:_____

All the words in each line have the same vowel sound except for one. Cross it out and write its letter in the blank at the beginning of the line. At the end of the line, write another word that has the same vowel sound as the word you crossed out. The first one has been done for you.

1. __t__   r. cause   s. small   ~~t. soil~~   u. haul   ___boil___
2. _____   c. crawl   d. crown   e. loud   f. house   _____
3. _____   b. blue   c. threw   d. too   e. crow   _____
4. _____   e. yard   f. tear   g. card   h. sharp   _____
5. _____   r. truth   s. could   t. book   u. good   _____
6. _____   c. earn   d. heard   e. bear   f. germ   _____
7. _____   m. voice   n. point   o. joy   p. soft   _____

Read the letters of the words you crossed out, from the bottom up, to see if you found the right answers.

ACTIVITY 22   Spelling Words With the "oo" Sound, as in "Moon"

Name:_____

Date:_____

Draw arrows from left to right to spell a word that makes sense in each sentence. Here's how to do it: M   G   U   N
U ↘ O → O ↗ S

1. Let's ride out to the sand

```
      d  o  n  e  r
   s  u  r  l  s   this weekend!
      m  i  f  a  d
```

2. Jake plays the

```
   w  u  y  n                    c  l  a  t  y
   t  a  b  s   and Jack plays the  f  r  u  n  e .
   s  n  r  a                    b  o  k  m  s
```

3. We're waiting for the court to

```
      r  o  n  t
   s  u  p  e   on the new law.
      m  a  l  d
```

4. When the president walks by, members of the military always

```
   y  e  l  p  r  m
   w  a  z  u  o  e .
   s  t  o  c  t  n
```

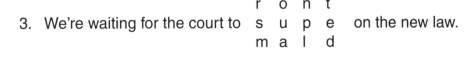

Now write sentences on your own paper using: produce, pollute, and attitude.

ACTIVITY 23 Spelling Words With the "aw" Sound, as in "hawk"

Name: _____

Date: _____

Read the clues to find words with the *aw* sound. Then write the words correctly in the blanks. Remember that the *aw* sound can be spelled in many ways.

1. something you drink through _ _ _ _ _
2. opposite of weak _ _ _ _ _ _ _
3. female offspring _ _ _ _ _ _ _ _
4. terrible _ _ _ _ _ _
5. to show approval by clapping _ _ _ _ _ _ _ _
6. month of the year _ _ _ _ _ _ _
7. people who see a show _ _ _ _ _ _ _ _ _
8. hot, brown drink _ _ _ _ _ _ _
9. sharp, curved nail on a bird _ _ _ _
10. clumsy _ _ _ _ _ _ _ _

On your own paper, write three sentences, using as many of these words as possible.

ACTIVITY 24 Spelling "ar" Words

Name: _____

Date: _____

Brainstorm! How many words of two or more syllables can you make using the word parts provided? Write your answers on the lines. Spell words in which the *ar* makes the sound we hear in *arm*.

Example: far_____: Answers: farmer, farther, farthest

1. gar _____: _____
2. char _____: _____
3. mar _____: _____
4. tar _____: _____
5. star _____: _____
6. bar _____: _____
7. war _____: _____

On your own paper, write a sentence for each word on any of the lines above.

ACTIVITY 25 Spelling Words With "or"

Name: _____

Date: _____

Fill in the blanks to correctly spell words with *or*.

3-letter words: o r __   __ o r

4-letter words: o r __ __   __ o r __   __ __ o r

5-letter words: o r __ __ __   __ o r __ __   __ __ o r __   __ __ __ o r

6-letter words: o r __ __ __ __   __ o r __ __ __   __ __ o r __ __   __ __ __ o r __

                __ __ __ __ o r

Challenge: Can you make a similar list for *er* words?

ACTIVITY 26 Spelling Words With "er" and "ur"

Name: _____

Date: _____

Circle the words that are spelled correctly. Cross out the words that are misspelled.

perfect	nurvous	alert	curtain
adverb	concurn	revurse	berglar
servey	return	terkey	expurt
observe	berden	herricane	survey
perple	transfer	turminal	person

On your own paper, make your own list of correct and incorrect words. Give it to a friend or family member. Can that person find all the mistakes?

ACTIVITY 27 Spelling Words That End With the "əl" Sound

Name:_____

Date:_____

Add *a* or *e* in the blanks to spell each word correctly.

1. Please use a clean tow__l when you shower.
2. He lost a nick__l down the drain.
3. The recipe uses one lev__l teaspoon of salt.
4. Always sign__l before you turn.
5. Learning to do ment__l math is fun!
6. I'd like to canc__l the newspaper.
7. My brother has a voc__l solo in the concert.
8. My dog is a true, loy__l friend.
9. I like to wear sand__ls to the beach.
10. *Geese* is the plur__l of *goose*.
11. Your mod__l of the White House is amazing!
12. My foot slipped off the ped__l.

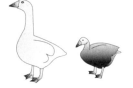

ACTIVITY 28 Spelling Words With Adjacent Vowels

Name:_____

Date:_____

Write a word for each clue in the crossword puzzle. Each word you spell will have two adjacent vowels that separate syllables, such as di-et.

1. make from nothing
2. destroy
3. hushed
4. era
5. three-sided polygon
6. related to sound or hearing
7. experiment

ACTIVITY 29 Spelling Words With "ie" and "ei"

Name:_____

Date:_____

Write the words from the word box under the right columns, using this spelling rule:
"*i* before *e* except after *c* or when sounding like *a* as in *neighbor* and *weigh*."

1. *i* before *e*

2. except after *c*

3. or when sounding like *a* as in *neighbor* and *weigh*

| believe |
| ceiling |
| eighty |
| thief |
| freight |
| chief |
| receive |
| vein |
| piece |
| lie |
| brief |
| weight |
| yield |
| deceive |

_____   _____   _____
_____   _____   _____
_____   _____   _____
_____   _____   _____
_____
_____
_____

Choose all the words in one column. Write a sentence for each one on another piece of papaer.

ACTIVITY 30 Spelling Words With "ie" and "ei"

Name:_____

Date:_____

Here are words that are commonly misspelled because of the *ie* and *ei* confusion. Write each one five times on the first line. Then write a sentence using each one on the second line.

1. believe _____

_____

2. friend _____

_____

3. receive _____

_____

4. neighbor _____

_____

5. eight _____

_____

ACTIVITY 31   Spelling Words With "ie" and "ei"

Name:_____

Date:_____

The spelling rule, "*i* before *e* except after *c* or when sounding like *a* as in *neighbor* and *weigh*" is right only part of the time. There are many exceptions. Write the words from the word box under the correct columns.

sleigh	friend	neither	niece	their	weird	perceive
beige	ancient	receipt	retrieve	grief	protein	conceited

1. *i* before *e*	2. except after *c*	3. when sounding like *a* as in *neighbor* and *weigh*	4. Exceptions
_____	_____	_____	_____
_____	_____	_____	_____
_____	_____	_____	_____
_____	_____	_____	_____
_____	_____	_____	_____

On your own paper, write a sentence using each word in column 4.

ACTIVITY 32   Spelling Words With "ie" and "ei"

Name:_____

Date:_____

Look at the spellings of each word. Circle the letter of the one that is spelled correctly.

1. U. neighbor   L. nieghbor
2. A. wieght   S. weight
3. I. recieve   E. receive
4. A. either   N. iether
5. R. foriegn   D. foreign
6. I. field   A. feild
7. C. leisure   P. liesure

8. T. friend   S. freind
9. H. beleif   I. belief
10. U. acheive   O. achieve
11. M. cieling   N. ceiling
12. A. vein   E. vien
13. R. height   T. hieght
14. S. riendeer   Y. reindeer

What's the best way to know if you're spelling these words correctly? To find out, write the letters of your answers, in order.

___ ___ ___   ___   ___ ___ ___ ___ ___ ___ ___ ___ ___ ___ !

ACTIVITY 33 Commonly Misspelled
Words: "usually"

Name:_____

Date:_____

Here's an exercise to make sure you don't usually have trouble spelling *usually*. Finish each sentence, using *usually* in your answer. Answers do not have to be true.

> *Example:* When it rains, I usually splash in the mud puddles.

1. When I travel, I _____.

2. When my pet is sick, it _____.

3. When I do my homework, I _____.

4. When I don't do my homework, I _____.

5. When I want to be kind, I _____.

6. When my teacher is sick, my classmates _____.

7. When my best friend comes over, _____.

8. When there's a snowstorm, my family _____.

ACTIVITY 34 Commonly Misspelled
Words: "tomorrow"

Name:_____

Date:_____

Don't wait until tomorrow to learn how to spell *tomorrow*. Do it today with this extra practice! Complete each sentence with one of these sets of words.:

Tomorrow I will   Tomorrow I might   Tomorrow I won't

1. _____ take out the garbage

2. _____ finish my homework.

3. _____ investigate something I'm curious about.

4. _____ sleep in.

5. _____ meet someone new.

6. _____ learn something new on the computer.

7. _____ make an important decision.

8. _____ do something to help someone else.

ACTIVITY 35 Commonly Misspelled Words: "probably"

Name: _____

Date: _____

You probably don't have trouble spelling *probably*, but if you do, here's some extra practice. In each blank, write either *probably does* or *probably doesn't*.

1. My bedroom _____ need to be cleaned.

2. The dog _____ need a bath; my little brother _____ need a bath.

3. The president _____ plan to visit my school soon.

4. A little green Martian _____ live in my backyard.

5. The Man in the Moon _____ really exist.

6. My latest invention _____ have a practical use.

7. My plan for the future _____ include becoming a millionaire.

8. My retirement plan _____ include living overseas.

ACTIVITY 36 Commonly Misspelled Words: "separate"

Name: _____

Date: _____

Practice spelling *separate* as you answer these questions. Use a complete sentence for each answer, which includes *separate* or *separately*. Write the answers on your own paper

1. What things should be separate in your grocery cart?

2. What things should be separate in your school cafeteria?

3. What things should be separate in your classroom?

4. What things should be separate in your community?

5. What things should be separate in the government?

6. What things should be separate in nature?

7. What things should be separate in your brain?

18

ACTIVITY 37   Review of Activities 29–36

Name:_____

Date:_____

Cross out the words in the box that are spelled incorrectly. Then write the remaining words in the blanks below so that the sentences make sense.

nieghbor
freind
neither
niece
weird
biege
ancient
recieve
retrieve
greif
conceited
usually
probaly
tommorow
seperate
field

1. My _____ and my nephew are both adorable.

2. _____ of them ever gets into trouble.

3. Their parents _____ buy them everything they want.

4. Last summer, they visited every Major League baseball _____ in the country.

5. On their next vacation, they will visit the _____ pyramids.

6. Because the two kids never fuss or forget their homework, some folks say they're a bit _____.

7. Because they have everything they want and aren't very friendly, others say they're _____.

ACTIVITY 38   Review of Activities 29–36

Name:_____

Date:_____

Circle the misspelled words in this paragraph. Rewrite the paragraph correctly on your own paper.

    I can't beleive I helped to catch a real theif, right in our own nieghborhood! It started when I left the dog kennel outside by mistake. Inside was a doggy protien treat. The door was propped open with a stick. I'd taken Doggy outside for a breif run, but then I'd walked him back inside the house and forgot about the kennel. (I am usualy not that forgetful.)

    I went to bed promptly at eihgt minutes after ten. (I always listen to the weather forecast on the nightly news before turning in. And since my little brother and I sleep in seperate rooms, I can stay up later than he can.) At ten twenty-eight, while I was still staring up at the cieling, there was a whang-bang-snap sound in the backyard. I jolted up in my bed and raced outside. Trapped inside the dog kennel was a gigantic raccoon! Immediately, I was joined by Mr. Pibbles from next door.

    "Congratulations, freind! You caught the nighttime bandit who is probaly responsible for stealing at least five of Martha's homemade boysenberry pies." (I wondered why anyone, or anything, would want any of those.) "I'm happy to give you the reward we've been offering," Mr. Pibbles exclaimed most enthusiastically.

    "What's the reward?" I asked.

    "It's a dozen boysenberry pies! I'll retrieve a peice for you right now. We'll bake the rest for you tommorow," he replied.

    This may sound wierd, but I don't think I'll forget and leave the kennel outside ever again.

ACTIVITY 39 Commonly Confused Words: "then/than"

Name:_____

Date:_____

Then is a word that means *next* or *at that time*.
  Example: First you wash, and then I'll dry.
Than is a word used for comparison.
  Example: I am taller than Peter.

Write *then* or *than* in each blank.

1. Herb was a faster runner _____ Rich, but Rich typed faster _____ Herb.

2. Herb asked Rich to race, and _____ Rich challenged Herb to a typing contest.

3. In one minute, Herb typed 20 words, and _____ Rich typed 55 words.

4. "Rich, why are you so much faster _____ I am?" asked Herb.

5. "Perhaps it's because I learned on a typewriter first and _____ I switched to a computer. Or maybe it's because I always warm up and _____ I type."

6. Herb replied, "I wish I was a faster typist. But at least I can beat you to the ice cream shop. What could be better _____ that?"

ACTIVITY 40 Commonly Confused Words: "quit/quiet/quite"

Name:_____

Date:_____

Quit means *to stop*, or *to leave one's work*.
Quiet means *making no sound*, *with little noise*, or *still*.
Quite means *completely* or *entirely*.

Answer each question with a complete sentence, using *quit*, *quiet*, or *quite* in each one.

1. I've had quite enough of political campaign ads. What things have you had quite enough of?

_____

2. What things should people quit doing? _____

3. What things are not quiet at all? _____

4. What things are too quiet? _____

5. What things are not quite right? _____

ACTIVITY 41 Commonly Confused Words: "already/all ready"

Name:_____

Date:_____

Already is an adverb that means *before now*.
   Example: She already had everything she needed for school.
All ready can be used as an adjective that means *completely prepared*.
   Example: He is all ready to go to the store.

Add *already* or *all ready* to each blank.

1. How can it _____ be time to go to bed, Mom?

2. I was _____ to start a movie!

3. It's only September, but I've _____ started Christmas shopping.

4. I'd like to be _____ for that holiday plenty early.

5. At seven o'clock, we were _____ to go to the concert, but it had _____ started.

6. We _____ heard about your illness, and we're _____ to help you!

On your own paper, write two sentences using *already* and *all ready* correctly.

ACTIVITY 42 Commonly Confused Words: "altogether/all together"

Name:_____

Date:_____

Altogether means *entirely*.
   Example: We're altogether certain we are in the right place.
All together means *in unison* or *gathered in one place*.
   Example: We decided all together that we would get a pet.

Decide if each sentence is correct. Put a check in the right blank.

		Right	Wrong
1.	It's not altogether true that our family never spends time together.	____	____
2.	We spend vacations all together every year.	____	____
3.	Next year, we have decided to do something all together different.	____	____
4.	We will stay here and go altogether to a different park every day.	____	____
5.	All together, the little children sang a silly song.	____	____
6.	It's altogether possible that it will rain today.	____	____
7.	We decided to buy Mom a gift all together.	____	____

21

ACTIVITY 43 Commonly Confused Words: Name:_____

"anyone/any one," and "everyday/every day" Date:_____

Anyone, as one word, is a pronoun that means *any person at all*.
      Example: Can anyone tell me the password?
Any one, as two words, refers to *one of many things in a group*.
      Example: Choose any one of the books in the library.
Everyday, as one word, is an adjective that means *ordinary*.
      Example: We are using the everyday glasses tonight.
Every day, as two words, is used as an adverb that tells *when*.
      Example: I comb my hair every day.

Write the best word in each blank from the four choices listed above.

1. I think _____ of those colors would look great on you!

2. The _____ drudgery of some jobs leads to boredom.

3. The policeman was looking for _____ who had witnessed the crime.

4. You should eat several servings of fruits and vegetables _____.

5. This painting is one of which _____ could be proud.

ACTIVITY 44 Commonly Confused   Name:_____

Words: "desert/dessert"   Date:_____

Desert can be pronounced two ways. It has two different meanings.
      a. The first pronunciation is /dĕz′ ərt/. This means *a hot, dry place*.
      b. The second pronunciation is /dĭ zûrt′/. With this prononunciation, the word
         means *to leave or abandon. Example:* The upset players deserted their
         team.
Dessert, with a double *s*, means *the last part of a lunch or dinner*. Often, it is sweet.

Write the correct word below. Then write *a* or *b* to tell which pronunciation of *desert* is correct.

1. Aunt Amy makes the best chocolate _____ (____).

2. We traveled out west to visit the Painted _____ (____).

3. On a long, hot journey through the _____ (____), several soldiers wanted

    to _____ (____) their unit.

4. Do you wonder what it would be like to live on a _____ed (____) island?

5. Before you _____ (____) the dinner table, how about some

    _____ (____)?

6. Watching a movie about life in the _____ (____) made me hot and thirsty!

ACTIVITY 45 Commonly Confused Words: "sometime/sometimes/some time"

Name:_____

Date:_____

Sometime, as one word, is an adverb that means *at an unidentified time*.
   Example: We should visit that museum sometime.
Sometimes, with an *s*, means *now and then*.
   Example: Sometimes it's fun to solve a crossword puzzle.
Some time, as two words, means *a span of time*.
   Example: Her teapot has been broken for some time now.

Complete each sentence, using the correct meanings as shown above.

1. Sometimes alligators _____.

2. It's been quite some time since I _____.

3. Sometime I would like to _____.

4. Sometimes store clerks _____.

5. I need some time to _____.

6. Sometime you and I could _____.

ACTIVITY 46 Commonly Confused Words: "loose/lose"

Name:_____

Date:_____

Loose means *not firmly attached*.
   Example: Would you like me to pull out your loose tooth?
Lose means *to misplace* or *to fail to win*.
   Example: I hope I don't lose my new watch. My team won't lose this game!

Write either *loose* or *lose* in each blank.

1. His bike slipped on the _____ gravel.

2. When her shoestring came _____, the ice skater tripped and fell.

3. You never want to _____ your wallet or your car keys.

4. My brother is so good at chess that he never _____s.

5. The handmade mat was very _____ly woven.

6. If the next batter hits a home run, the home team will _____ the game.

7. When things are tough, don't _____ hope that things will get better.

ACTIVITY 47 Commonly Confused Words: "accept/except"

Name: _____

Date: _____

Accept means *to take what is offered*.
    Example: I'm happy to accept your gift.
Except means *leaving out*, or *other than*.
    Example: Everyone is going except Tim.

Write either *accept* or *except* in each blank.

1. Late at night, I _____ phone calls from no one _____ my parents.

2. Some folks are offended if you don't _____ their kindnesses.

3. Please put all these ingredients in the salad, _____ for the olives.

4. _____ for the little boy who couldn't swim, everyone enjoyed the pool party.

5. I have to _____ my disability and make the best of it.

6. Susan will _____ a very big honor tonight at the awards ceremony. No one

    knows about it _____ her teacher.

ACTIVITY 48 Commonly Confused Words: "lay/lie" and "set/sit"

Name: _____

Date: _____

Lay means *to put something down*.
    Example: Please lay down your knife while you're chewing.
Lie means *to recline* or *be situated*.
    Example: I lie down every day for a quick afternoon nap.
Set means *to place something somewhere*.
    Example: He set the groceries on the table.
Sit means *to move into a seated position*.
    Example: My dog sits every time I ask him to.

Circle the correct word in each sentence.

1. Please (set / sit) down while I (set / sit) out my pictures for you to see.

2. Mary planned to (lay / lie) a cloth on the table and then (set / sit) her best dishes on it.

3. George will (lay / lie) in bed all day because he has a fever.

4. Since I just (set / sit) out all the chairs for the party, I think I need to (lay / lie) down.

5. If a little child learns to (set / sit) still, he can listen and learn a lot!

ACTIVITY 49 Commonly Confused Words: "through/thorough"

Name:_____

Date:_____

Through is a preposition that means *from one end to the other*. It has one syllable.
    Example: We walked through the tunnel.
Through can also mean *at the end of*, or *done*.
    Example: She stayed until the play was through.
Thorough is an adjective that means *all that is needed; complete*. It has two syllables.
    Example: The detectives did a thorough search of the room.

Write either *through* or *thorough* in each blank.

1. Why is Gertrude searching _____ her dresser drawers?

2. She is certainly being very _____.

3. Is she all _____ yet?

4. Did her _____ search turn up anything interesting?

5. She is reading _____ her will again.

6. I think she wants to add more gifts to it before she is _____.

7. Gertrude is so _____ about all of her business affairs.

ACTIVITY 50 Commonly Confused Words: "breath/breathe," "conscience/conscious"

Name:_____

Date:_____

Breath is a noun that means *air taken into to the lungs and let out again*. It is pronounced with a short *e*.
    Example: I tried to hold my breath for 30 seconds.
Breathe is a verb that means *to take air into the lungs and let it out again*. It is pronounced with a long *e*.
    Example: When you have a cold, you should not breathe on others.
Conscience means *the awareness of right and wrong*. It is a noun.
    Example: The little boy had a troubled conscience after he stole the candy.
Conscious means *awake and able to think*. It is an adjective.
    Example: She was badly injured, but she is still conscious.

Write a sentence using each of these tricky words correctly.

1. breath _____

2. breathe _____

3. conscience _____

4. conscious _____

ACTIVITY 51 Review of Activities
39–42

Name: _____

Date: _____

Write one word from the word box in each blank. You will not use all the words.

quit	then	already	altogether	quite
than	all ready	all together	quiet	

1. Dad said, "It's too _____ in here. I think you're up to something!"

2. "I'd rather you tell me the truth _____ make up a story," he said.

3. "It's been _____ awhile since you guys were in trouble."

4. "Are you _____ certain there isn't something you

    want to say?" asked Dad.

5. "If you're sure, _____ I'm sure."

6. Then we decided to spill the beans _____. It wasn't fun.

7. "I've _____ forgiven you," said Dad. "Thanks for telling the truth."

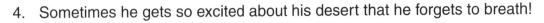

ACTIVITY 52 Review of Activities
39–50

Name: _____

Date: _____

Circle every misspelled or misused word in these sentences. Write each correction above the sentence. Some sentences may need more than one correction.

1. My neighbor realy likes desert. He never gets enough apple pie.

2. Chet wants pie everyday. Any one can see that's not healthy.

3. He gets quiet enough sugar just from his breakfast cereal!

4. Sometimes he gets so excited about his desert that he forgets to breath!

5. Once, when he became ill, Chet actually did loose his appetite.

6. Some times Chet will just set and look at chocolate bars.

7. Than he walks away from the table and goes to lie down.

8. Chet is trying to lose weight. All ready he has lost 18 pounds.

ACTIVITY 53   Review of Activities
39–50

Name: _____

Date: _____

Circle every misspelled or misused word in this story. Write the correct word above the wrong one.

Let me tell you about our sixth-grade field trip. It was quit a trip! First, everyone loaded in the bus at six a.m. Than we drove for two hours. Everyone wondered if the trip would be worth the drive. By the end of the day, we were all together certain it was!

We met Governor Fisher. We met all the members of his cabinet, accept for the secretary of state. We had to set very quitely during some important meetings. We dined in the governor's mansion. These are not every day activities for us!

When we climbed back on the bus, the teachers asked if we were already for one more stop. The bus driver winked, and the next thing we knew we were at Frosty Ice Cream Parlor. Every one of us graciously excepted a free ice cream cone, compliments of the governor!

ACTIVITY 54   Review of Activities
29–50

Name: _____

Date: _____

Circle every misspelled or misused word in this story. Rewrite the story correctly on your own paper.

The cheif of police was puzzled. Everyday for a week now, a mysterious caller phoned him with the same message:

"Set down at noon, Chief. We're coming to see you!" What was he to think? He didn't usualy recieve such strange calls.

He asked his fellow officers to wiegh in on the subject. What would they do? The results were mixed.

Finaly, on Thursday night, the chief reached his decision. "The voice sounds muffled but friendly. I'll probaly regret this, but tommorow I will be already. I'll be setting at my desk at noon. But my deputies will also stand ready if anything wierd should happen.

Friday at noon, there was a knock on his door. "Surprise!" yelled his grandkids altogether. "We thought we'd never get you here at the right time. We've been waiting all week to give you a surprise birthday party!"

The chief took a deep breathe. If he hadn't been at his desk at noon today, he would have had a bad conscious for a very long time.

ACTIVITY 55 Homophones:
"to," "too," "two"

Name:_____

Date:_____

Write *to*, *too*, or *two* in each blank.

> Remember:
> *To* is a preposition that means *in a direction toward*.
> *Too* is an adverb that means *also* or *more than enough*.
> *Two* is a number.

1. We should go _____ the bank.

2. We have _____ much money _____ keep stuffing it under our mattress.

3. You know, _____ million one-dollar bills makes for a lumpy mattress!

4. There are some good reasons _____ keep a little cash in the house, but if we have _____ much around, someone might steal it.

5. So let's talk _____ the bank manager and see what kind of account we should open.

6. After we deposit all this cash, maybe we can go _____ the movies, unless the tickets are _____ expensive.

7. If the ticket prices are reasonable, maybe we could even watch _____ movies.

ACTIVITY 56 Homophones:
"to," "too," "two"

Name:_____

Date:_____

You can never have too much practice with the homophones *to*, *too*, and *two*!

Cross out each incorrect word.
Write the correct word above it.

> Remember:
> *To* is a preposition that means *in a direction toward*.
> *Too* is an adverb that means *also* or *more than enough*.
> *Two* is a number.

It didn't take Nick to long to learn how two use the computer.

At the very young age of too, he crawled up on his mom's desk chair and found the power switch. He clicked on the mouse and in to seconds, he was playing a fast-paced game and reading an online encyclopedia. Nick's mother walked into the room. She was to astonished to speak.

When he was three, Nick's mom was writing a book called *How Two Parent a Genius.* Nick tried not to be to picky, but he circled all her spelling mistakes!

ACTIVITY 57 Homophones: "there," "their," "they're"

Name:_____

Date:_____

Write *there*, *their*, or *they're* in each blank.

> **Remember:**
> *There* means *at* or *in that place*. It also indicates the existence of something, as in: *There is a house over there.*
> *Their* means *belonging to them.*
> *They're* means *they are.*

1. Is _____ any reason why I should go to bed early?

2. Yes, I believe _____ is!

3. It's because the Switherspoons have invited us to _____ house for a gourmet meal tomorrow.

4. _____ personal chef, Pierre, is preparing an eight-course meal, and _____ very kind to invite us.

5. I'm told _____ very selective about whom they invite over to _____ home.

6. Okay, but why do I have to go to bed early tonight if we're not going over to _____ house until tomorrow night?

7. Sweetheart, _____ invitation is for breakfast at 5 A.M.!

ACTIVITY 58 Homophones: "there," "their," "they're"

Name:_____

Date:_____

Write a paragraph about one of the topics below. Use all three homophones (*there, their,* or *they're*) at least once in your paragraph.

> **Remember:**
> *There* means *at* or *in that place*. It also indicates the existence of something, as in: *There is a house over there.*
> *Their* means *belonging to them.*
> *They're* means *they are.*

- How people succeed in business
- How siblings drive each other crazy
- How great babysitters act
- How someone survives on a deserted island
- How kids become great spellers

Proofread your paragraph. Then give it to a friend to check for mistakes.

ACTIVITY 59 Homophones:
"threw/through"

Name: _____

Date: _____

Threw is the past tense of *throw*.
> *Example:* Yesterday, the pitcher threw a no-hitter.

Through is a preposition that means *from one end to the other*.
> *Example:* We walked through the tunnel.

Through can also mean *at the end of* or *done*.
> *Example:* He is through with the dishes.

Write *threw* or *through* in each blank.

1. My friend _____ away a perfectly good cell phone.

2. He said he was all _____ with it, but I wasn't so sure.

3. I took it from the trash and made a call. The call went right _____.

4. In fact, I got _____ to Buckingham Palace!

5. My friend said he also _____ away the details of his calling plan, so he had no idea what it would cost to put that call _____ to England.

6. "Don't worry," I said. "The queen just said she'd put any calls from this number on her account, up _____ the end of the year!"

- -

ACTIVITY 60 Homophones:
"break/brake"

Name: _____

Date: _____

Break often means *to come apart*, as in: *How did my beautiful vase break?* It also has several other meanings. Consult your nearest dictionary.

Brake is *a device for stopping a vehicle*, or *the act of using it*.
> *Example:* Please brake when you see kids in the street.

Write *break*, *brake*, or *brakes* in each line.

1. The car needs to have _____ repairs done.

2. You have to _____ a few eggs to make an omelet.

3. Hey, give me a _____! I didn't mean to sit on your new hat!

4. I was able to leave work early today because I did not take a lunch _____.

5. There was a communication _____ down, so I did not receive the report.

6. Wes is hoping to _____ the previous record in the mile run.

7. The truck's _____ failed and caused an accident that shut down the highway for hours.

ACTIVITY 61 · Various Homophones

Name:_____

Date:_____

Circle the correct homophone for each sentence.

1. I hope you're not (board / bored) with the executive (board / bored) meeting.

2. Every time a thunderstorm approaches, my Aunt Maggie gets a (creak / creek) in her knee.

3. We watched the kite (sore / soar) over the fields and (creak / creek).

4. Suzanne's heroic (feat / feet) should not go unrewarded!

5. We're hoping that the (sores / soars) on Grandpa's (feet / feat) and (heals / heels) soon (heal / heel).

6. The (main / mane) event at the camp this year is horseback riding.

7. My horse's (main / mane) and tail were so long, I braided them!

ACTIVITY 62 · Various Homophones

Name:_____

Date:_____

Find a homophone for each word listed here. Circle it in the puzzle and write it in the blank. Beware! Many of the homophones are spelled much differently than their partners.

1. kernel _____
2. coo _____
3. shoot _____
4. coral _____
5. draft _____
6. marshall _____
7. side _____
8. peer _____
9. toad _____
10. wrapped _____
11. flare _____
12. yolk _____
13. we _____
14. phase _____
15. dough _____

```
C L A R O H C S
Y O K E I X I L
C O L R U G T A
D O E O H W P I
E E U E N E A T
W T D P I E R R
O U E Z A F L A
T H G U A R D M
Q C K R I A L F
```

On your own paper, write sentences correctly using both words in numbers 2, 4, 6, 8, and 10.

ACTIVITY 63 Various Homophones

Name: _____

Date: _____

Write correct answers in the blanks for each set of clues.

1. chose correctly/honored visitor: _ _ _ _ _ _ _ / _ _ _ _ _

2. soft animal hair/an evergreen tree with flat needles: _ _ _ / _ _ _ _

3. tightly wrapped bundle of hay/money paid to free someone from jail:

   _ _ _ _ / _ _ _ _

*4. the location of something/the ability to see: _ _ _ _ / _ _ _ _ _ _

*5. blood vessel that carries blood to the heart/of no use:

   _ _ _ _ / _ _ _ _

*6. leather strap attached to a horse's bit/period of time a king rules:

   _ _ _ _ / _ _ _ _ _

7. not with another person, single/something borrowed: _ _ _ _ / _ _ _ _

Bonus: *On your own paper, write a third homonym and definition for each of these pairs.

ACTIVITY 64 Various Homophones

Name: _____

Date: _____

These words have homophones with which you may not be familiar. Use a dictionary or other reference book to find a homophone for each word here. Then write a sentence for each homophone. The first homophone has been provided.

1. away   _____

   aweigh   _____

2. lean   _____

   _____

3. birth   _____

   _____

4. ball   _____

   _____

5. sweet   _____

   _____

ACTIVITY 65 Various Homophones

Name:_____

Date:_____

Pull apart two homophones from each set of letters. You will not need to change the order of the letters. Example: didyee = die/dye Note: Sometimes there are three homophones to untangle. The items with * are bonuses.

1. seceedde   _____

2. whholollyy   _____

3. kngnenewuw   _____

4. soswaoredrd   _____

5. tthhrroonwen   _____

*6. fplholcoxks   _____

7. secelllearr   _____

8. uearrnn   _____

*9. eyywoeewu   _____

10. wriririgtgtehht _____

11. totoawded   _____

*12. sceereriaall   _____

On your own paper, write sentences using one pair of homophones.

ACTIVITY 66 Homophones:
"capital/capitol"

Name:_____

Date:_____

Capital refers to

1. a city where the government of a state or country is located
2. money or property that is invested to make more money
3. an uppercase letter

Capitol refers to

4. With a capital *C*, the building in Washington, D.C., where the U.S. Congress meets
5. With a lowercase *c*, the building in which a state legislature meets.

Write the correct word in the blank in each sentence. Write the number of its definition in the blank at the end of the sentence.

1. Little Tommy found it easier to write _____ letters than small ones. _____

2. A journalist reported from inside the U.S. _____ building. _____

3. The developer raised more _____ before starting the project. _____

4. Lansing is the _____ of Michigan. _____

5. Hundreds of reporters gathered inside the _____ building to hear the state senator's announcement. _____

33

ACTIVITY 67 Homophones: "principle/principal"

Name:_____

Date:_____

Principal often refers to   1. first in order of importance (adjective)
                               2. the head of a school (noun)
                               3. a person who is an important member of something (noun)
                               4. the primary sum of money, apart from interest (noun)
Principle often refers to   5. a basic truth or law (noun)
                               6. a rule of personal conduct (noun)

Write the correct word in the blank in each sentence. Write the number of its definition in the blank at the end of the sentence.

1. Newton discovered the _____ of gravity. _____

2. The _____ reason for the trip is to attend Clint's wedding. _____

3. Our new _____ this year is Mr. Matteson. _____

4. As a matter of _____, I try to be polite to everyone. _____

5. In 10 years, Jassem doubled the _____ on his investment. _____

6. The _____ person in the business is my uncle. _____

ACTIVITY 68 Homophones: "stationary/stationery"

Name:_____

Date:_____

Stationary refers to   1. not changing position; remaining still
                          2. not capable of being moved
                          3. not changing with time
Stationery refers to   4. writing paper and envelopes

Write the correct word in the blank in each sentence. Write the number of its definition in the blank at the end of the sentence.

1. The drawbridge was replaced by a _____ bridge. _____

2. I ordered new _____ for our company. _____

3. The windsock was _____ throughout the windless morning. _____

4. The price of gold is often _____ for several years. _____

Write a sentence of your own for *stationary* and *stationery*.

_____

_____

ACTIVITY 69   Editing to Correct
Easier Homophones

Name: _____

Date: _____

Circle all the mistaken homophones in this story. Then rewrite it correctly on another peace of paper.

You wood knot believe this unless it happened two ewe! I was sitting buy myself, clothes

to a tree. I planned to reed a book. Butt suddenly, sum pointy thing poked me in my shoulders. I

jumped up in fright. I was to scared to look behind me to sea what it was. But finally, I did. It was

two giant mousse, with big antlers and everything! I didn't no I was

near there home. Yew probably think I'm a lyre, but it really happened

to me. Sew it could happen to you, two! Beware...

Bonus: Did you find the error in the directions?

ACTIVITY 70   Editing to Correct
More Difficult Homophones

Name: _____

Date: _____

Circle all the mistaken homophones in this story. Then rewrite it correctly on another piece of paper. Hint: There are 10 errors.

We took a tour through the nation's capital. It was suite to see where

Congress meets to rite laws. To see the principals of democracy in action

was awesome. We were holy in awe threw the entire tour. We watched a

debate in the House. Their was a reel difference of opinion on a new tacks.

One person was so tide to his opinion that you would have had to move him

off the floor with a bulldozer!

ACTIVITY 71 Contractions

Name: _____

Date: _____

It's is the contraction for *it is*. We use the apostrophe in place of the *i* that was deleted.

I'll is the contraction for *I will*. This time, two letters—*w* and *i*—were omitted.

Write the contraction for each of these word pairs. Put the apostrophe in the place where letters were deleted.

1. he would   _____
2. she is   _____
3. you are   _____
4. I am   _____
5. there had   _____
6. will not   _____
7. who has   _____
8. they are   _____
9. does not   _____
10. must not   _____
11. there would   _____
12. she will   _____
13. Which two sets of words form the same contraction? _____

ACTIVITY 72 Contractions

Name: _____

Date: _____

Circle the correct word for each sentence. Write it again in the blank at the end of the sentence.

1. (Who's / Who'se) afraid of the big bad wolf? _____
2. (Thats / That's) been a good question for years. _____
3. (I've / Iv'e) been working on the railroad. _____
4. (Youv'e / You've) been working on the railroad for how long? _____
5. It (doesn't / dosen't) matter who you are. _____
6. (You're / Your) still a very important, precious person. _____
7. (Its / It's) about time you realized that! _____
8. If it (wern't / weren't) true, I (wouldn't / would'nt) have told you.

_____   _____

ACTIVITY 73   Contractions

Name: _____

Date: _____

Rewrite each sentence to get rid of double negatives.

Wrong: She couldn't never get to work on time.

Correct: She couldn't ever get to work on time. OR She could never get to work on time.

1. We couldn't get no sleep last night. _____
   _____

2. Mrs. Axe's cat wouldn't stop no howling. _____
   _____

3. That wasn't no way to spend the night. _____
   _____

4. Mrs. Axe says there isn't nothing to be done. _____
   _____

5. My dad says there isn't no truth to that. _____
   _____

6. He bought us all earplugs that won't let no sound through. _____
   _____

ACTIVITY 74   Editing to Correct
Contractions

Name: _____

Date: _____

Put an "X" by the sentences that contain errors. Rewrite those sentences correctly on another piece of paper. Put an "OK" by the sentences that are okay.

_____ 1. Its about time you learned how to make applesauce.

_____ 2. First, wash the apples and cut them until their in small chunks.

_____ 3. Next, you'll want to cook the apples until they are no longer firm.

_____ 4. Don't forget to stir them often, so they don't stick to the pan.

_____ 5. Then scoop the soft apples into a food mill to squeeze the
   pulp away from it's skin.

_____ 6. When your all done squeezing the pulp, stir the sauce.

_____ 7. Add some sugar until the sauce isn't too tart.

_____ 8. Finally, pour some applesauce out into a dish. If its not too hot, eat and enjoy!

ACTIVITY 75 Prefixes That Identify Quantity

Name: _____

Date: _____

Some prefixes show quantity, or how much. For each meaning given, list at least one prefix. On the second line, spell two words that use the prefix(es) you listed.

Example: one   <u>uni, mono</u>   <u>unicycle, monotone</u>

1. half   _____   _____

2. two   _____   _____

3. eight   _____   _____

4. hundred   _____   _____

5. three   _____   _____

6. four   _____   _____

7. many   _____   _____

- -

ACTIVITY 76 Prefixes That Mean "not"

Name: _____

Date: _____

Many prefixes change the meaning of the base word to its opposite. For example, adding *un-* to *welcome* forms *unwelcome* and means *not welcome*.

Choose the correct prefix from the following list to add to each of the words below: *il-*, *ir-*, *un-*, *im-*, *dis-*, *mis-*, *in-*. Write the new word in the blank with its correct spelling. Use a dictionary, if necessary.

Example: <u>communicate</u> + <u>mis</u> = <u>miscommunicate</u>

1. cover + _____ = _____   2. connect + _____ = _____

3. logical + _____ = _____   4. responsible + _____ = _____

5. comfort + _____ = _____   6. possible + _____ = _____

7. regular + _____ = _____   8. believable + _____ = _____

9. ability + _____ = _____   10. legal + _____ = _____

11. patient + _____ = _____   12. expensive + _____ = _____

ACTIVITY 77   Prefixes: "extra-," co-," "ex-," "circum-," "in-," "auto-," "inter-"

Name: _____

Date: _____

Write the letter of each meaning next to the prefix it matches. Use what you know about the words in the word list to help you. Then spell two more words that begin with the same prefix.

Prefixes
a. self   b. with, together   c. out   d. outside, beyond   e. around   f. into   g. between, among

_____ 1. *ex:* exhale, exhaust, exit, _____, _____

_____ 2. *auto:* automobile, autograph, autopilot, _____, _____

_____ 3. *co:* cooperate, coexist, cosign, _____, _____

_____ 4. *in:* inside, insole, inject, _____, _____

_____ 5. *extra:* extraterrestrial, extracurricular, _____, _____

_____ 6. *inter:* international, interplanetary, _____, _____

_____ 7. *circum:* circumference, circumvent, _____, _____

ACTIVITY 78   Assorted Prefixes

Name: _____

Date: _____

Write one word from the box in each blank so that each sentence makes sense. Watch your spellings as you recopy each word.

pro-labor
synchronize
prologue
paramedic
prearrange
supervise
correspond

1. You'll need to _____ the small children at the party.
2. Will your vacation _____ with your wife's vacation?
3. When the singer's _____ was finished, everyone was ready for the concert to begin.
4. Each _____ goes through extensive medical training.
5. The _____ union put on a big rally for the political candidate.
6. The dancing duo practices for endless hours to _____ their movements.
7. Some folks _____ their funerals.
8. Which two words in the box have prefixes that mean *with*?

_____, _____

39

ACTIVITY 79 Assorted Prefixes

Name: _____

Date: _____

What words can be formed with these prefixes and roots? Draw lines to connect the prefixes that can be added to the root words. Then write all the words you make on the lines.

Prefixes   **Roots**

pre   way   _____   _____

post   form   _____   _____

trans   game   _____   _____

sub   port   _____

              test

ACTIVITY 80 Assorted Prefixes

Name: _____

Date: _____

Add a prefix to the word in each sentence so that it makes sense. Write the new word in the blank. Remember that when prefixes are added, the spelling is not changed, even if double consonants result. Example: *re + entry = reentry*.

1. I am highly (satisfied) _____ with this food, so I want a refund.

2. The journalist quoted an (named) _____ source when writing his story.

3. After I put the woolen sweater in the washer, it was very (shapen) _____.

4. Since my services seem to be (needed) _____, I think I'll go home.

5. The judge told the jury to (regard) _____ the witness's last comment.

6. I want to be sure to (pay) _____ my loan on time.

7. My (biography) _____ is sure to be a best

    seller, because my life has been so remarkable!

ACTIVITY 81   Suffixes: When to Double a Final Consonant

Name:_____

Date:_____

If a word ends with one consonant and has just one vowel before the consonant, we double the consonant before we add endings that begin with vowels, such as -*ed* and -*ing*.

Examples: hop → hopped   cut → cutting

We do not add consonants to words that end in two consonants.

Examples: collect → collected   find → finding

Add these word parts. Spell the resulting word on each line.

1. stop + ing = _____

2. laugh + able = _____

3. control + ed = _____

4. begin + ing = _____

5. sleet + ing = _____

6. knot + ing = _____

7. plan + ed = _____

8. regret + ed = _____

9. quit + ing = _____

10. sleep + ing = _____

ACTIVITY 82   Suffixes: Adding to Words That End in "y"

Name:_____

Date:_____

When a suffix is added to a word ending with a consonant and a *y*, there are two rules:

• Keep the final *y* when adding a suffix that begins with *i*.
  Example: studying
• Change the *y* to *i* with all other suffixes.
  Example: studied

In the puzzle, find the correct spellings of these words to which suffixes have been added. Write the words that you find on the blanks below.

M	A	R	R	Y	I	N	G	Q	U
Y	Y	G	N	I	Y	T	P	M	E
Y	L	S	T	A	Y	I	N	G	B
L	C	I	T	H	U	M	W	Q	U
I	R	O	R	E	K	O	A	T	S
D	Y	E	S	G	R	E	E	N	I
E	I	N	K	R	N	I	C	E	E
E	N	V	Y	O	W	U	O	X	R
R	G	I	L	L	P	O	H	U	S
G	N	I	Y	F	S	I	T	A	S
G	N	I	Y	F	I	L	A	U	Q

1. satisfy _____

2. busy _____

3. empty _____

4. worry _____

5. qualify _____

6. cry _____

7. greedy _____

8. stay _____

9. hungry _____

10. marry _____

11. mystery _____

ACTIVITY 83 Adding Suffixes to Words That End in Silent "e"

Name:_____

Date:_____

When we add a suffix that begins with a vowel (*a, e, i, o, u*) to a word that ends with a silent *e*, we usually drop the silent *e*.

  Examples: joke + ed = joked   divide + ing = dividing

When we add a suffix that begins with a consonant, we usually keep the *e*.

  Examples: excite + ment = excitement

Cross out each misspelled word and write the correct spelling above it.

1. bounce + ing = bouncing   2. disable + ed = disabled

3. creative + ly = creativly   4. write + ing = writeing

5. forgive + ness = forgiveness   6. life + less = lifless

7. pollute + ing = polluteing   8. rejoice + ing = rejoicing

9. trample + ed = trampled   10. manage + ing = managing

11. imagine + ing = imagineing   12. observe + ance = observance

---

ACTIVITY 84 Adding Suffixes to Words That End in Silent "e"

Name:_____

Date:_____

When we add a suffix that begins with a vowel (*a, e, i, o, u*) to a word that ends with a silent *e*, we usually drop the silent *e*.

  Examples: excite + ed = excited

When we add a suffix that begins with a consonant, we usually keep the *e*.

  Examples: excite + ment = excitement

Write the new word in each blank.

1. arrange + ed _____ arrange + ment _____

2. believe + ed _____ believe + ing _____

3. care + ing _____ care + less _____

4. safe + ly _____ safe + ty _____

5. forgive + ness _____ forgive + ing _____

6. name + ly _____ name + ing _____

ACTIVITY 85 Adding Suffixes to Words That End in Silent "e"

Name: _____

Date: _____

Usually, when we add a suffix that begins with a vowel to a word that ends with a silent *e,* we drop the silent *e.* When we add a suffix that begins with a consonant, we usually keep the *e.* But there are several common words that are exceptions to the usual rules.

Can you spot the exceptions in the activity below? Circle the correct spelling of each word. Use a dictionary to double check your answers.

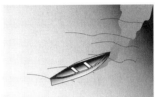

1. truly   truely
3. possibley   possibly
5. argument   arguement
7. wholely   wholly
9. aweful   awful
11. canoeing   canoing

2. wisedom   wisdom
4. width   wideth
6. terribley   terribly
8. judgement   judgment
10. manageable   managable
12. milage   mileage

Now write the correct spellings of each of these words on your own paper.

ACTIVITY 86 Suffixes: "-ly," "-ily"

Name: _____

Date: _____

We can add *-ily* or *-ly* to an adjective to tell in what manner something happened. For example, if someone spoke in a very loud voice, we might say he spoke *loudly.*

For each sentence, write a word that ends in *-ly* or *-ily*.

1. Shawn sneezed very (loud) _____.
2. He didn't mean to sneeze so (noise) _____.
3. He had been working so (reliable) _____ before the sneeze.
4. Now he (thoughtful) _____ considered going on break.
5. People were looking at him (accusing) _____, as if he'd done something wrong.
6. He acted (decisive) _____, by sending an e-mail apology to all.
7. Shawn then (wise) _____ went back to work.

ACTIVITY 87 Suffixes: "-ful"

Name:_____

Date:_____

When we add *full* to any word, we drop the second *l*.
    Example: cheer + full = cheerful
Sometimes we have to change a *y* to *i*:
    Example: beauty + ful = beautiful

Write at least one *-ful* word for each topic. One example is given for you.

1. a summer evening: *peaceful*_____   2. a rainbow   _____

3. a hot pepper _____   4. a lawn   _____

5. a circus clown _____   6. a rattlesnake _____

7. a new puppy _____   8. a doctor   _____

9. a difficult task _____   10. a rocking chair _____

Using a dictionary, check the spellings of the words you wrote.

ACTIVITY 88 Suffixes: "-less," "-ness"

Name:_____

Date:_____

The suffix *-less* means *without; not having.* For example, *hopeless* means *without hope.* The suffix *-ness* means *the quality of.* So, *happiness* means *the quality of being happy.* Write a word in each sentence, adding either *-less* or *-ness* to the base word provided. Remember to watch the spellings of words that end in *y* or silent *e.*

1. Her heart was filled with (heavy) _____ as she waved goodby to her son.

2. As he walked off into the (dark) _____, she hoped she'd prepared him for the future.

3. Sometimes, the poor boy looked so (help) _____.

4. She'd feel awful if he were (care) _____ and wound up (penny) _____.

5. The mother thought again that her son bore a (like) _____ to his father.

6. She knew she'd spend at least one (sleep) _____ night.

7. "Honey, come to bed," called the woman's husband. "For (good) _____ sake. He's only moving into the basement, and he's 22 years old!"

ACTIVITY 89 Suffixes: "-able," "-ible"

Name:_____

Date:_____

The suffixes -*able* and -*ible* mean *can be.*
   Example: If a sweater can be washed, it is *washable.*

Unscramble the letters below to spell an -*able* or -*ible* word. Write the word you form on the long line. Then match each word to one of the definitions by writing the correct letter on each short line.

_____ 1. glubaleha   _____   a. something that can be seen

_____ 2. liveabbeel   _____   b. something that can be removed

_____ 3. blsiive   _____   c. something that can be laughed at

_____ 4. leccotlebli   _____   d. something that can be managed

_____ 5. blayepa   _____   e. something that can be paid

_____ 6. vomrleeba   _____   f. something that can be believed

_____ 7. beengamala   _____   g. something that can be collected

ACTIVITY 90 Suffixes: "-ion," "-tion," "-ation"

Name:_____

Date:_____

Write one word from the word box that makes sense in each sentence.

| decision |
| division |
| examination |
| explanation |
| occupation |
| punctuation |
| suggestion |
| television |

1. My father's _____ is farming.

2. May I make a _____ about our project?

3. Many people use little or no _____ in their e-mail messages.

4. What's your favorite _____ show?

4 / 9 =

5. Mrs. Rice's _____ of the _____ problem helped us to solve the rest of the math problems.

6. After a careful _____ of the evidence, the jury reached a _____.

ACTIVITY 91 Suffixes: "-ant," -"ent"

Name:_____

Date:_____

The word endings -ant and -ent mean *one who* or *a thing that*. For example a *servant* is *one who serves*. A *coolant* is *a thing that cools*. The endings -ant and -ent change verbs to nouns.

Write a noun ending in -ant or -ent for each of these verbs. Then use it in a sentence.

Example: claim → claimant   A claimant is someone who claims something.

Sentence: The claimant of the lottery jackpot came forward today to collect his prize.

1. assist   _____   _____

2. preside   _____   _____

3. inform   _____   _____

4. immigrate _____   _____

5. account   _____   _____

6. reside   _____   _____

ACTIVITY 92 Suffixes: "-ance," "-ence"

Name:_____

Date:_____

Adding -ance or -ence to a word usually changes a verb to a noun. For instance, if something *appears*, we say that it makes an *appearance*.

Add an *a* or an *e* to each word below. Use a dictionary if you need help.

1. differ __ nce   2. clear __ nce   3. occurr __ nce

4. audi __ nce   5. obedi __ nce   6. import __ nce

7. perform __ nce   8. disturb __ nce   9. accept __ nce

10. refer __ nce   11. assist __ nce   12. depend __ nce

13. exist __ nce   14. observ __ nce   15. disappear __ nce

On your own paper, write sentences for three of the words above.

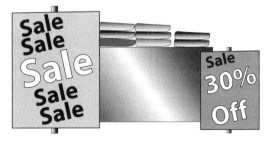

ACTIVITY 93 Review of Prefixes and Suffixes

Name:_____

Date:_____

Use these word parts to spell at least eight new words. Then write sentences for four of your words.

Prefixes	Base Words	Suffixes	Your Words:
un	legal	able/ible	_____ _____
mis	change	ance/ence	
il	direct	ful	_____ _____
dis	help	ion/tion	
	imagine	ly	_____ _____
	appear		
	prefer		_____ _____

Sentences:

_____

_____

_____

_____

ACTIVITY 94 Review of Prefixes and Suffixes

Name:_____

Date:_____

Add prefixes and/or suffixes to each word in parentheses so that each sentence makes sense.

There were so many (spell) _____ errors in the book that I could not

read it. (Possible) _____ the book was about an upset artist who was (satisfy)

_____ with a picture he'd painted. On the other hand, the book may have

been a (discuss) _____ of the (appear) _____ of a pitcher. At

any rate, I think it's (reason) _____ to say that the book needs to be (written)

_____!

ACTIVITY 95   **Compound Words**

Name: _____

Date: _____

A **compound word** is one that is made up of two parts, each of which can stand as a word on its own. Are the words below compound words or not? Check the correct box for each one. Watch out for prefixes and suffixes that aren't really words!

		Yes	No				Yes	No
1.	themselves	☐	☐	8.	cartwheel		☐	☐
2.	throughout	☐	☐	9.	astonishment		☐	☐
3.	whirring	☐	☐	10.	commotion		☐	☐
4.	windbreak	☐	☐	11.	headquarters		☐	☐
5.	shuffled	☐	☐	12.	fingernail		☐	☐
6.	streamline	☐	☐	13.	fairground		☐	☐
7.	redwood	☐	☐	14.	mournfully		☐	☐

If you answered *yes*, write the two words that form each compound on your own paper.

ACTIVITY 96   **Compound Words**

Name: _____

Date: _____

Each square contains an 9-letter compound word. Find it by starting with the center letter, then reading either clockwise or counterclockwise around the square. Write the compound words in the blanks.

```
O O N          P A V          N C H          H I  P
N A F          O E E          U L T          S S  P
R E T          R D S          E M I          E C  A
```

1. _____   2. _____   3. _____   4. _____

```
E R T          G R E          R E H          O O K
A B S          R E E          A W O          D W C
K F A          E V N          E S U          C H U
```

5. _____   6. _____   7. _____   8. _____

On another piece of paper, write sentences for four of these words.

ACTIVITY 97 Compound Words

Name: _____

Date: _____

Brainstorm to see how many compound words you can make by filling in the blanks.

1. _____ bread   2. _____ storm   3. _____ light
   _____   _____   _____
   _____   _____   _____
   _____   _____   _____
   _____   _____   _____

4. _____ time   5. _____ worm   6. _____ stone
   _____   _____   _____
   _____   _____   _____
   _____   _____   _____
   _____   _____   _____

Now double check in the dictionary to see if the words you made should be written as one word or two. Rewrite any words that need to be corrected.

ACTIVITY 98 Compound Words
With Silent "e"

Name: _____

Date: _____

When we combine two small words to make a compound word, we do not drop the silent *e*.

   Example: bare + foot = barefoot, not barfoot!

Write a compound word that makes sense in each sentence. Each one will contain a silent *e*.

1. The _ _ _ e _ _ _ _ _ at the pool was glad he did not have to rescue anyone this week.

2. Our janitor empties the classroom _ _ _ _ e _ _ _ _ _ _ every night.

3. We just had our _ _ _ _ e _ _ _ paved, so we have to park on the street.

4. Grandma always says that Grandpa is a true _ _ _ _ _ e _ _ _ because he opens the door for her.

5. What could be better than eating hot dogs and popcorn at the _ _ _ e _ _ _ _ game?

6. Our _ _ _ e _ _ _ _ for finishing the project was moved up. I hope we can finish in time!

7. I know I put my car keys _ _ _ e _ _ _ _ _ in this house! Now I wish I could find them!

49

ACTIVITY 99 Compound Words

Name: _____

Date: _____

Match these small words to form 14 compound words. Be sure to use each word listed here only once.

clock	foot	time	cart	work	fare	light
walk	snow	air	room	tail	man	keeper
watch	wheel	fore	lamp	moon	rattle	ball
warn	snake	class	cotton	stop	side	post

_____ _____

_____ _____

_____ _____

_____ _____

_____ _____

_____ _____

_____

ACTIVITY 100 Two-Word and
Hyphenated Compounds

Name: _____

Date: _____

Some compounds are written as two words. Some are written with hyphens. Use a dictionary to double check the compounds in this list. Then write them correctly in the right category.

highschool	milesperhour	boobytrap	halftruth	seatbelt
selfserve	flashlight	babysitter	grandfather	exmanager
greatgrandchild	editorinchief	fireworks	southwest	

A. One word **B. Two words** **C. Hyphenated**

_____ _____ _____

_____ _____ _____

_____ _____ _____

_____ _____ _____

_____

ACTIVITY 101 Syllabication

Name:_____

Date:_____

Write a word in each square of the chart. The word should begin with the letter on the top and contain the number of syllables shown at the left. You may use a dictionary. Some examples are given for you. Give yourself 5 points for each box you fill. Can you score at least 70 points?

	R	I	G	H	T
1		ice			
2					
3	regular				
4					

Number of points: _____

ACTIVITY 102 Syllabication

Name:_____

Date:_____

Here are two simple rules for dividing words into syllables:

    A. In a compound word, the first word is usually the first syllable: sun – shine

    B. If the word begins with a prefix, the prefix is usually the first syllable: un – paid

Rewrite each of these words, separating them by syllables. Then write the letter of the rule you used.   *Example:*   carport: car – port, A

1. redone _____ ____
2. suitcase _____ ____
3. shoreline _____ ____
4. copay _____ ____
5. backyard _____ ____
6. eyebrow _____ ____
7. rewrite _____ ____
8. biceps _____ ____
9. housework _____ ____
10. birthday _____ ____
11. disarm _____ ____
12. software _____ ____

ACTIVITY 103 Syllabication

Name: _____

Date: _____

Here are two rules for dividing two-syllable words with two consonants in the middle:

- A word is always divided between double consonants: lad – der   bub – ble
- Most words are divided between two consonants when each makes its own sound:
  bar – gain   bas – ket

Rewrite the words in bold, separating them by syllables.

Our camp director used a lot of **wisdom** when he **composed** the **written** rules for the **swimming** pool. His rules **assure** both **campers** and parents that kids will be safe. No one can **afford** to have **unsafe** things **happen** in the water! If campers break the rules or argue about the rules, the director can easily **settle disputes** and carry out **justice**.

1. _____
2. _____
3. _____
4. _____
5. _____
6. _____
7. _____
8. _____
9. _____
10. _____
11. _____
12. _____

ACTIVITY 104 Syllabication

Name: _____

Date: _____

Note these important rules about dividing words into syllables:
- When a single consonant falls between two vowels, the consonant usually goes with the first vowel, if the vowel makes the short sound: sol – id   rap – id
- The consonant usually goes with the second vowel if the first vowel makes a long sound: la – bor   cra – dle
- Do not separate consonant digraphs: chick – en

Decide if each word is divided correctly. Circle the letter in the correct column.

	Right	Wrong			Right	Wrong
1. or – phan	I	A	9. hyp – hen	F	G
2. pa – per	N	S	10. ba – by	H	P
3. mys – elf	R	T	11. em – ploy	A	E
4. ec – hoes	A	H	12. not – ice	S	T
5. ho – tel	E	I	13. pho – to	E	N
6. bug – le	L	C	14. spid – er	W	R
7. u – nit	O	M	15. ro – bot	I	O
8. nep – hew	E	U	16. re – cent	A	S

Write the letters of your answers in order to spell the answer to this riddle: Where do you eat lunch if you have a cold? __ __   __ __ __   __ __ __ __ __ - __ - __ __ __ __ __ __!

ACTIVITY 105 — Syllabication

Name: _____

Date: _____

Find ten words with two syllables in the puzzle, all beginning with the letter J. Circle the words in the puzzle. Write them on the blanks, dividing them correctly into syllables.

_____

_____

_____

_____

_____

_____

_____

_____

_____

_____

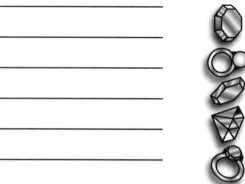

L	R	A	U	G	A	J	N	O
J	K	J	A	C	K	P	O	T
A	E	L	U	C	K	L	I	T
S	L	A	A	Z	E	R	T	E
M	B	O	L	W	E	A	C	K
I	M	Y	E	O	Y	B	N	C
N	U	J	A	W	U	A	U	A
E	J	O	K	E	R	S	J	J

ACTIVITY 106 — Syllabication

Name: _____

Date: _____

Don't divide between two adjacent vowels if they carry one sound.
Examples: be – lieve   a – loud
Do divide between two adjacent vowels when each carries a sound.
Examples: bus – i – est   ra – di – o

Rewrite each word, dividing it correctly into syllables. **Tip**: Some words contain only one syllable and do not need to be divided at all.

1. creative _____

2. tourist _____

3. reaction _____

4. shriek _____

5. nuisance _____

6. briefly _____

7. heroic _____

8. auction _____

9. cause _____

10. material _____

11. receivable _____

12. bureau _____

ACTIVITY 107 Syllabication

Name: _____

Date: _____

Here are some very long words that you may encounter in your reading. Even though the words may look extremely difficult, many times you can figure them out if you read each one slowly, syllable by syllable.

Read each word carefully and try to sound it out. Write the number of syllables you believe each word contains. Then look up each word in the dictionary to see if you are right.

1. negotiations _____

2. commercialization _____

3. oceanographer _____

4. communicative _____

5. transcontinental _____

6. biochemistry _____

7. polyunsaturated _____

8. binomial _____

9. monolingual _____

10. incredulous _____

11. cacophony _____

12. omnivorous _____

On your own paper, write sentences for three of these big words.

ACTIVITY 108 Syllabication

Name: _____

Date: _____

In each row, one word is divided incorrectly. Circle it. Then write it correctly in the blank.

1. a – pol – o – gy   am – ateur   am – bi – tion   _____

2. count – er – fe – it   cu – ri – ous – i – ty crit – i – cism   _____

3. dic – tion – ar – y   dis – app – ear   dis – turb – ance   _____

4. eas – i – est   ex – pe – rience   en – vi – ron – ment _____

5. go – vern – ment   guar – an – tee   gen – u – ine   _____

6. hap – pi – ness   hi – sto – ry   hu – mor – ous   _____

7. im – me – diate   in – no – cent   in – de – pen – dence _____

8. la – zi – ness   lead – er – ship   leg – i – slat – ion _____

54

ACTIVITY 109 Plurals

Name:_____

Date:_____

Singular means *one of something*. **Plural** means *more than one*. We make most plurals by just adding *s*.

    Example: one letter ⟶ two letters

If the noun ends with *s*, *ch*, *sh*, *x*, or *z*, we usually add *es* to make it plural.

    Example: one brush ⟶ a set of brushes

Write the correct plural for each noun in the cross-word puzzle.

Across	Down
1. watch	1. walrus
5. gorilla	2. horizon
6. buzz	3. pasture
7. nap	4. elm
8. step	6. bus

ACTIVITY 110 Plurals

Name:_____

Date:_____

To make a plural of a noun that ends in *y*:
- Add *s* if the letter in front of the *y* is a vowel: toy ⟶ toys
- Drop the *y* and add *ies* if the letter in front of the *y* is a consonant: penny ⟶ pennies

Write the correct plural for each word in the blanks.

1. dictionary _____   2. story _____

3. decoy _____   4. country _____

5. bay _____   6. treaty _____

7. party _____   8. alley _____

9. trolley _____   10. category _____

11. worry _____   12. study _____

ACTIVITY 111 Plurals

Name: _____

Date: _____

To make some nouns that end with *f* or *fe* plural, change the *f* to *v* and add *es*.
Example: knife ⟶ knives
Caution: *safe*, *bluff*, and *waif* do not follow this rule. For these words, just add *s*.

Read each sentence carefully. First, decide if the bold word is singular or plural. Then, decide if it's spelled correctly. On the blank, write either OK or the corrected form of the word.

1. Every fall when the **leafs** _____ begin to turn, two **churchs** _____

    join together for a huge bake sale to raise funds for the homeless.

2. Husbands and **wives** _____ bake breads, cookies, cakes, and pies.

3. Some huge **loaves** _____ of bread are cut in **halfs**. _____

4. One year, **thieves** _____ broke in and stole both baked goods and cash.

5. Now, the money is kept in the **safes** _____ in both churches.

6. At the end of the sale, folks are quite pleased with **themselfs**. _____

ACTIVITY 112 Plurals

Name: _____

Date: _____

Nouns ending in *o* preceded by a vowel usually form the plural by adding *s*.
Example: patio ⟶ patios
Nouns ending in *o* preceded by a consonant usually form the plural by adding *es*.
Example: hero ⟶ heroes

Read the sentences and decide which word from the word box makes the most sense in each sentence. Then spell its plural form and write it correctly in the blank.

patio
potato
radio
ratio
tomato
tornado

1. My brother's favorite food is mashed _____ with gravy.

2. In math class, we're studying fractions, _____, and percents.

3. We were all told to turn our car _____ to the same station to hear music that

    was synchronized with the fireworks display.

4. My grandpa grows the biggest, reddest _____ in the whole county!

5. Uncle Jeff builds customized decks and _____ for new homes.

6. _____ swept through the countryside, causing much

    destruction.

ACTIVITY 113 Plurals

Name: _____

Date: _____

Irregular plurals are those that don't follow any of the usual rules or patterns. You need to memorize them or look them up in a dictionary.

Write the plural of each noun in the diagram.

1. ox
2. mouse
3. foot
4. moose
5. corps
6. fungus
7. goose
8. tooth
9. crisis

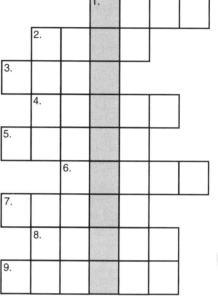

Read the word going down the shaded squares. It forms one acceptable way to spell the plural of *octopus*!

ACTIVITY 114 Plurals

Name: _____

Date: _____

Circle every mistake with plurals in the paragraph. On your own paper, write the correct form of each word you circle.

Three gooses flew into a shopping mall full of men, womans, and childs. They squawked and honked. The animals waddled through aisles of shoe, dress's, and slacks. They flapped by coats, scarves, gloves, and mitten's. Finally, they flew into a huge tank full of fish and turtles, sending splashs of water onto books, toys, ferns, and cactusies.

Gasps could be heard throughout the mall. "How could this have happened? Why were the doors all left open? Why didn't some guardes shoo them back outside?"

Finally, some wise guyes supplied the answers. "Well, folks, maybe the geese just needed some new cloths!"

57

ACTIVITY 115   Plurals

Name:_____

Date:_____

There are certain nouns that name something that is not usually counted, like *sand* or *courage*. These non-count nouns do not usually form plurals.

Can you unscramble these non-count nouns? Write each one on the blank.

1. gruas _____	2. bytaue _____
3. grane _____	4. virles _____
5. retuna _____	6. snesphiap _____
7. voel _____	8. levgar _____
*9. litengleceni _____	*10. oshca _____

*Bonus words

- -

ACTIVITY 116   Plurals

Name:_____

Date:_____

Choose 12 of these 15 unrelated nouns. Then use the plural of those 12 nouns to write a goofy story of your choice. Be sure to use the correct spelling of those plurals.

_____

_____

_____

_____

_____

_____

_____

batch
buffalo
dirt
flour
group
hitch
jury
library
pony
smudge
square
sheep
swine
wharf
zoo

ACTIVITY 117   Singular Possessives

Name: _____

Date: _____

A **singular possessive** noun shows that a single person or thing owns something else. Usually we form singular possessive nouns by adding *'s* to the noun.

> *Example:* a boy's shirt, the moon's shape

Write the possessive form of each noun in the blank. Then write a sentence for five of these singular possessives on your own paper.

1. dentist _____

2. tiger _____

3. newspaper _____

4. match _____

5. laptop _____

6. straw hut _____

7. vegetable _____

8. classroom _____

9. zookeeper _____

10. balloon _____

ACTIVITY 118   Singular Possessives

Name: _____

Date: _____

When a singular word ends in *s*, we usually add *'s* to that word.
> *Example:* James's final <u>story</u> was very interesting.

Choose a word from the box. Write the word in its possessive form on the blank. Underline the object that belongs to the possessive noun, as in the example above.

wilderness
Royal Highness
Janis
Boris
business
Congress
mattress
Arkansas

1. The new _____ tag read "Do not remove."

2. _____ main duty is to write and pass laws.

3. One _____ motto is "Save Money, Save Jobs."

4. "Excuse me, but your _____ crown needs to be polished."

5. We hiked in the _____ mountains and swam in its rivers.

6. _____ and _____ children were named Jano and Boro.

7. _____ tourist bureau made commercials to encourage folks up north to visit during the winter.

59

ACTIVITY 119   Plural Possessives

Name:_____

Date:_____

When a plural noun ends in *s*, we add only an apostrophe to the word.
Example: cats ⟶ cats' food
When a plural noun does not end in *s*, we add *'s*.
Example: men ⟶ men's cars

Rewrite each phrase using a plural possessive noun. The first one has been done for you.

1. the textbooks that belong to the students   *the students' textbooks*_____

2. the envelopes that belong to the secretaries   _____

3. the cheese that belongs to the mice   _____

4. the coats that belong to the women   _____

5. some income that belongs to workers   _____

6. the enamel on your teeth   _____

ACTIVITY 120   Singular and Plural Possessive Pronouns

Name:_____

Date:_____

Be sure to write possessive pronouns correctly.
    Correct: Was the shirt hers?   *Incorrect:* Was the shirt her's?
Remember that *it's* only has an apostrophe when it is used as a contraction for *it is*.

Circle the numbers in front of any sentence that is already correct. Fix errors in the other sentences by crossing out the faulty words and writing in the correct ones above the sentence.

1. The responsibility for the problem was your's.

2. It wasn't Sue's fault or Mike's fault.

3. Now your problem has become our's, and we want you to fix it.

4. Please discuss this with your boss's assistant before anyone gets hurt.

5. The problems solution is so simple.

6. I'm surprised that some of the other genuis's didn't think of it.

7. All you have to do is answer your own phone calls, instead of answering everyone else's!

ACTIVITY 121　Plurals and Possessives

Name: _____

Date: _____

Identify each underlined word by writing the correct letter or letters above it:

S – singular　　　　P – plural　　　　SP – singular possessive　　　　PP – plural possessive

1. All the kids are hoping to go to the Brillo <u>Brothers'</u> <u>circus</u>.

2. Some <u>kids</u> say <u>theirs</u> is the best circus in the world!

3. They know this <u>circus's</u> <u>clowns</u> are the best.

4. Their <u>animals'</u> <u>performances</u> are also excellent.

5. The <u>Brillos</u> hire amazing trapeze <u>acrobats</u> to perform daring <u>stunts</u>.

6. Once an <u>acrobat's</u> <u>swing</u> broke, and she fell over forty <u>feet</u>!

7. Thankfully, the safety <u>net's</u> location was perfect to catch the <u>acrobat's</u> fall.

ACTIVITY 122　Plurals and Possessives

Name: _____

Date: _____

Use the meaning of the sentence to decide which spelling inside each set of parentheses is correct. Circle the word that is right for each sentence.

1. When (its / it's) the right time to shop, you must do it!

2. Don't wait for tomorrow when the best (sales / sale's) date is today.

3. The sales clerks each predict that (theirs / their's) will be the busiest department.

4. I just found some great (buys / buy's) on some beautiful (clothes / clothes').

5. I bought two (dollar's / dollars') worth of socks. Believe it or not, I got six (pairs / pairs') of polka-dotted ones for that price!

6. The three new (sweater's / sweaters') sequins are quite dazzling.

7. Mom says my new pajama (shirts / shirt's) neon flashing lights might be a bit much.

8. My new gym (shoes / shoes') whistling shoelaces are my favorite acquisition.

ACTIVITY 123 **Plurals and Possessives** Name:_____

Date:_____

Spell the form of each word that is requested, using the abbreviations shown. Then use the word correctly in a sentence.

P – plural   SP – singular possessive   PP – plural possessive

box

1. P _____   _____

2. SP _____   _____

3. PP _____   _____

journey

4. SP _____   _____

5. PP _____   _____

it

6. SP _____   _____

ACTIVITY 124 **Special Plurals and** Name:_____

Date:_____

Possessives

Names and numbers can be tricky when it comes to possessive forms and the use of apostrophes. Here are some guidelines you can use:

- Plurals are generally formed by adding *s* or *es*:   girls, Smiths, Joneses
- Plural possessives are formed by adding an apostrophe: girls', Smiths', Joneses'
- Remember, personal pronouns do not use apostrophes: ours, **not** our's
- Plurals of numbers and letters are formed by adding *'s*:
  Examples: The answer to the problem contained three 4's.
  The word Mississippi is spelled with four i's.

Insert apostrophes where needed in this paragraph.

Your penmanship needs a lot of work. You need to remember to cross all your ts and dot all your is. When you write zs, they should not look like 2s. Have you ever read Betsy Fishers papers? Try to get your writing to look more like hers. All of the Fishers have great handwriting. In fact, all of the Fishers handwriting exceeds most of the teachers handwriting I have seen. The Fishers certainly write better than the doctors I know. If you work hard, better penmanship can definitely be yours!

ACTIVITY 125 Capitalization

Name: _____

Date: _____

We always capitalize the first word of every sentence, the pronoun *I*, and proper nouns.

Read each sentence starter. Rewrite it with correct capitalization, and finish the sentence.

1. when i read shel silverstein's book, i thought…

   _____

2. the twins, jenn and joe, are going to…

   _____

3. my favorite play is…

   _____

4. the best place to go on vacation would be…

   _____

5. i would travel 500 miles to hear…

   _____

ACTIVITY 126 Capitalization

Name: _____

Date: _____

Both proper nouns and proper adjectives are capitalized.

Try to think of three such words for each category listed here. Work with a friend if you need help. Remember to use correct capitalization.

1. Specific places and geographical regions, such as Lake Superior

   _____ _____ _____

2. Landmarks, such as the Golden Gate Bridge

   _____ _____ _____

3. Historical events and documents, such as the United States Constitution

   _____ _____ _____

4. Nationalities and their languages, such as Italian

   _____ _____ _____

5. Organizations and associations and their members, such as the Rotary Club or the Rotarians

   _____ _____ _____

ACTIVITY 127 Capitalization

Name: _____

Date: _____

Capitalize the names of days of the week, months of the year, and specific holidays, such as *Christmas* and *Kwanzaa*. Do not capitalize general words, such as *my birthday* or *next year*.

Write a short answer to each question using proper capitalization.

1. What are three holidays in February? _____

2. In what month do you start school? _____

3. What day of the week is tomorrow? _____

4. What day of the week was yesterday? _____

5. In what month were you born? _____

6. What is the first holiday of the year? _____

7. What is the last holiday of the year? _____

8. What is the next holiday on your calendar? _____

ACTIVITY 128 Capitalization

Name: _____

Date: _____

Follow the directions to find the answer to a riddle.

Up, Up, And away!	oregon	big holes	christopher columbus	milky way	yom kippur
caleb miller	Through The Looking Glass	china	jupiter	shelby brown	brooklyn bridge
thanksgiving	all over	ohio river	santa claus	The Sound And The Fury	old faithful
statue of liberty	pacific ocean	st. patrick's day	captain hook	labor day	Australia

1. Cross out all the names of people who should be capitalized but aren't.
2. Cross out all the names of places and landmarks that should be capitalized but aren't.
3. Cross out the names of holidays that should be capitalized but aren't.
4. Cross out all titles containing mistakes in capitalization.

Read the words in the remaining spaces to find the answer to this riddle:

Q: What do you get if you cross an elephant and a kangaroo ?

A: _____   _____   _____!

64

ACTIVITY 129 Capitalization

Name: _____

Date: _____

Capitalize the titles of people when they precede the proper names.
   Example: Professor John Marshall   Uncle Gary
Do not capitalize them when they follow the name or are used alone.
   Example: John Marshall, a professor   my uncle

Circle every letter that needs to be capitalized.

1.   every saturday i like to help my grandma.

2.   sara's dad has a conference with principal jones at noon today.

3.   president billings just resigned his position at the university.

4.   reverend patrick smith will give the address on friday.

5.   uncle joe, aunt jill, and grandpa dole all came to my birthday party.

6.   the attorneys listened as judge parsons gave them instructions.

7.   my great-grandfather was a senator from rhode island.

ACTIVITY 130 Capitalization

Name: _____

Date: _____

Capitalize the first word in the greeting and closing of a letter. Capitalize the names of streets, cities, and states.

Rewrite this letter on another piece of paper, correcting all the mistakes in capitalization.

4678 w. elm dr.
sometown, ak
nov. 3, 2007

dear sally,

       thanks for inviting me to your house for thanksgiving. unfortunately, mom and dad said that we can't make the trip to alaska this year. i always have fun hanging out with you and my other alaskan cousins, but my parents said that'll have to wait. instead of flying to alaska, I guess we're going to swim to tahiti for our turkey. go figure!

sincerely,
ryan

ACTIVITY 131   Capitalization

Name:_____

Date:_____

We capitalize the first word in a quotation, if it is the beginning of the sentence.
Capitalize *The* in this quotation, but not *and*:
"The popcorn is too salty," said the customer, "and I don't want to pay for it!"

Rewrite each of these sentences on your own paper with correct capitalization.

1. "every time I come to your theater," the customer complained, "your popcorn stinks!"
2. "today, it's too salty. last week, it was cold," he continued. "next week, I expect it will be burnt!"
3. the manager replied, "sir, I can see we have a problem here, and I'd like to correct it."
4. "nothing, and I mean nothing," the customer began, "can make up for the damages I've suffered. I had to watch an entire three-hour movie with popcorn that was too salty!"
5. "do you think," the grumbling man continued, "that i'll just pretend everything's okay and keep coming back here week after week?"
6. "perhaps this will help," offered the manager. "we'll give you a year's supply of rental movies at your nearest video store. that way, you can watch your movies at home!"

ACTIVITY 132   Proofing for Capitalization and Spelling Errors

Name:_____

Date:_____

Rewrite this paragraph on your own paper. Correct all errors in capitalization and spelling.

dad says i need a haircut. (i guess when i couldn't see my diner plate, dad figured it was time to do somthing.) anyway, i'm going to ned's shop tommorrow morning. its always an interesting expereince when i go their. once ned was giving a haircut to king omar of omarzia. another time, he was shaveing off the beard of doctor doolittle. the last time i was there (I beleive it was last april), ned was triming the hair on the back of a gorilla. i wonder what will happen tommorow!

ACTIVITY 133   Caledar Words:
Days of the Week

Name: _____

Date: _____

Be sure to use correct spelling when you are writing the days of the week. Also capitalize the first letter of each day. Solve these riddles and write the correct day of the week for each one.

1. In three days, it will be the day after Sunday. What day is it today? _____

2. Yesterday was two days before Tuesday. What day is it today? _____

3. One week ago, it was two days before Friday. What day is it today? _____

4. One week from today will be five days after Thursday. What day is it today? _____

5. Tomorrow will be two days after Wednesday. What day is it today? _____

6. Today starts with *S*, but it doesn't have an *R*. What day is it today? _____

7. If you did all the others correctly, there's only one day left. What is it? _____

On your own paper, write the seven days in chronological order, beginning with Sunday.

ACTIVITY 134   Calendar Words:
Months of the Year

Name: _____

Date: _____

Write the name of the month in which each of these special days occurs. Use correct spelling and capitalization.

1. Halloween _____

2. St. Patrick's Day _____

3. Labor Day _____

4. Presidents' Day _____

5. Mother's Day _____

6. Martin Luther King, Jr., Day _____

7. Father's Day _____

8. Independence Day _____

9. Thanksgiving _____

10. Christmas _____

11. What are the two months left over? _____ _____

On another piece of paper, write the names of the 12 months, in chronological order.

ACTIVITY 135 Calendar Words:
Days and Months

Name:_____

Date:_____

Supply the missing consonants in the names of the days and months below.

1. A u _ u _ _

2. _ o _ _ a _

3. _ u _ e

4. _ u e _ _ a _

5. _ e _ e _ _ e _

6. _ e _ _ u a _ _

7. A _ _ i _

8. _ _ u _ _ _ a _

9. _ e _ _ e _ _ a _

10. _ a _ u a _ _

11. _ o _ e _ _ e _

12. _ a _ _ _

13. _ u _ _ a _

14. O _ _ o _ e _

15. _ a _ u _ _ a _

16. _ _ i _ a _

17. _ e _ _ e _ _ e _

18. _ u _ _

ACTIVITY 136 Calendar Words:
Holidays

Name:_____

Date:_____

Write two special days that occur in each month. Be sure to use correct spelling and capitalization. A few answers are supplied for you.

January	February	March
_____	_____	_____
_____	_____	_____
April	**May**	**June**
_____	_____	_____
_____	_____	_____
July	**August**	**September**
_____	*First day of school*	_____
_____	*Birthday of Neil Armstrong*	_____
October	**November**	**December**
_____	_____	_____
_____	_____	_____

ACTIVITY 137 Number Words

Name: _____

Date: _____

Watch your spelling as you follow these instructions.

A. Copy the number words in order from least to greatest value:

1. _____ 7. _____

2. _____ 8. _____

3. _____ 9. _____

4. _____ 10. _____

5. _____ 11. _____

6. _____ 12. _____

B. Copy the number words in alphabetical order:

1. _____ 7. _____

2. _____ 8. _____

3. _____ 9. _____

4. _____ 10. _____

5. _____ 11. _____

6. _____ 12. _____

| eight |
| fourteen |
| thirty |
| sixty |
| twenty |
| twelve |
| five |
| thirteen |
| nineteen |
| forty |
| fifteen |
| hundred |

ACTIVITY 138 Number Words

Name: _____

Date: _____

Use a hyphen between the tens word and the ones word:
    32: thirty-two   87: eighty-seven
Use commas in number words just as you would when writing the numeral:
    59,186: fifty-nine thousand, one hundred eighty-six

Write these numbers in words, using the rules above and correct spelling.

1. 3,067 _____

2. 42,918 _____

3. 831,056 _____

4. 1,572,437 _____

5. 167,845 _____

6. 99,099 _____

ACTIVITY 139 Number Words

Name:_____

Date:_____

Use the code to spell the number words. Then add the numbers together and write the sum words.

1.   * ^ ! $ #   _____

   + * & * $ #   _____

                       _____

? = E	! = R
* = F	% = S
↗ = H	$ = T
& = I	• = U
) = N	¶ = W
^ = O	< = X
# = Y	

2. % & < $ #   _____

   + $?)   _____

                      _____

3. * ^ • ! $? ?)   _____   4. $ ¶ ?) $ #   _____

   + $ ↗ ! ? ?   _____   + $ ¶ ?) $ #   _____

                      _____   _____

ACTIVITY 140 Number Words

Name:_____

Date:_____

Remember:
Cardinal number: 3 – three
Ordinal number: 3rd – third

Follow the directions.

1. Start with the ordinal word for 3. _____

2. Add the ordinal word for 5. _____

3. Add the ordinal word for 7. _____

4. Subtract the three letters that spell the cardinal number for 10. _____

5. Subtract four letters that are the consonants in *served*. _____

6. Subtract two *h's*. _____

7. Rearrange the remaining letters to spell an ordinal number word:

    __ __ __ __ __ __ __

ACTIVITY 141 Abbreviations: Titles

Name:_____

Date:_____

We use the standard abbreviations *Dr.*, *Mr.*, *Mrs.*, *Ms.*, and *Rev.* for titles immediately before proper names: Rev. Jim Bowles

After names, we use abbreviations such as *M.D.*, *D.D.S.*, and *Sr.*: Paul Jones, Sr.

Notice the correct placement of periods in these examples.

Also note that if there is no proper name used, then the titles should be spelled out:

Right: I went to the doctor. Wrong: I went to the Dr.

Each sentence below has at least one mistake in the use of titles and abbreviations. Circle the errors. Rewrite the sentences correctly on your own paper.

1. Our neighbor, the Sr. Mr. McDonald, has a big farm.
2. Mr. McDonald, Jr, is also known as James McDonald, DDS.
3. Mrs McDonald is actually Rev. McDonald.
4. The youngest McDonald hopes to someday become Gen McDonald.
5. I'd say that Old McDonald, Sr, has quite a farm!

ACTIVITY 142 Abbreviations:

Days and Months

Name:_____

Date:_____

Review the correct abbreviations for days and months. Then use a calendar for this year to look up the day and month of each special day listed. An example is done for you.

1. 3rd Monday in 1st month *Mon., Jan.18*_____
2. 2nd Tuesday in 2nd month _____
3. 4th Thursday in 11th month _____
4. 1st Sunday in 4th month _____
5. 2nd Saturday in 10th month _____
6. 3rd Friday in 8th month _____
7. 1st Wednesday in 3rd month _____
8. 4th Tuesday in 7th month _____

As you look at the calendar, what date of this year are most looking forward to?

_____

ACTIVITY 143 Abbreviations:

Addresses

Name:_____

Date:_____

We use many abbreviations when writing street addresses. Write the correct abbreviation, in-cluding a period, for each of these words.

1. Street _____
2. Avenue _____
3. Boulevard _____

4. Drive _____
5. Court _____
6. Parkway _____

7. Lane _____
8. Road _____
9. Trail _____

We use two-letter postal codes for the names of states. Ohio = OH   Hawaii = HI
Notice these abbreviations do not contain periods.
Write the two-letter postal code for each of these.

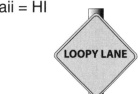

10. Your state _____

11. Three states nearest yours _____ _____ _____

12. Five states that touch the Mississippi River _____ _____

_____ _____ _____

ACTIVITY 144 Abbreviations:

Measurements

Name:_____

Date:_____

There are 18 units of standard and metric measure-ment inside this puzzle. Circle all the words you find, and write them on the lines below. Then write the abbreviation for each unit of measurement. Note: One unit does not have an abbreviation.

R	E	T	I	L	O	L	I	K
E	R	C	A	R	E	T	E	M
T	C	U	P	I	R	Z	A	I
E	J	N	F	A	N	R	O	L
M	N	O	U	P	G	C	W	L
I	O	Q	I	O	A	R	H	I
T	T	N	L	U	L	E	M	G
N	T	I	X	N	L	T	A	R
E	K	Q	J	D	O	I	R	A
C	D	R	A	Y	N	L	G	M

_____   _____

_____   _____

_____   _____

_____   _____

_____   _____

_____   _____

_____   _____

_____   _____

_____   _____

ACTIVITY 145 Abbreviations and Acronyms

Name: _____

Date: _____

An *abbreviation* is a shortened form of one word. We use the abbreviations *Inc.*, *Bros.*, and *Co.* when it is part of the official name of a business. We use periods after abbreviations. If the period for an abbreviation is at the end of a sentence, only one period is used.

Example: One of the biggest moving firms in San Diego is Barker Bros., Inc.

An *acronym* is formed by the initials of a title two or more words long. We use acronyms for organizations, corporations, and government agencies. No periods are used with acronyms.

Examples: New York Police Department ⟶ NYPD

Decide how many periods are needed in each sentence. Write the number on the blank. Then add the periods.

_____ 1. Mr Smith works for the AFL-CIO

_____ 2. Frank White, DDS, used to play for the NFL

_____ 3. My aunt is the president of Think Tank, Inc

_____ 4. William S Quinton hopes to work for the FBI

_____ 5. Pvt Mark Brown is in the USMC

ACTIVITY 146 Abbreviations: Review

Name: _____

Date: _____

When we send e-mails, we often write informally. We use *A.M.* or *P.M.*, *&, etc.* and other abbreviations more than we would in formal writing.

Rewrite this letter, which is full of abbreviations, so that it is correct for a more formal letter. Use another piece of paper for your new letter.

Dear Gene,

This A.M. I heard back from the dr. My test results are all ok. That's really good news. I'm sure I'll save a lot of $$$ if I don't have to go back to see the doc again!

BTW, yesterday was great. It was at least 70° outside. Becca & I flew our kites about 100 ft. before the lines snapped.

Tomorr. I'm going to take Becca to meet the rev and we'll set our wedding date.

See ya,

Tom

ACTIVITY 147 Spelling List A–C

Name: _____

Date: _____

There are many words that are commonly misspelled by people of all ages. If you can memorize these, you will find yourself ahead of most fifth- and sixth-graders and even many adults. Here are 20 words that begin with the letters *A*, *B*, and *C*.

absence	chocolate	accidentally	conscience	appearance
committee	boundary	conscientious	beginning	achieve
believe	column	character	attendance	calendar
accommodate	amateur	acquaintance	continuous	convenience

On another piece of paper, rewrite these words in alphabetical order. Add three words of your own beginning with *A*, *B*, or *C* that you sometimes misspell. Then keep your list to study!

- -

ACTIVITY 148 Spelling List D–F

Name: _____

Date: _____

There are many words that are commonly misspelled by people of all ages. If you can memorize these, you will find yourself ahead of most fifth- and sixth-graders and even many adults. Here are 20 words that begin with the letters *D*, *E*, and *F*.

decision	definitely	desperately	develop	different
dissatisfy	doesn't	eighth	embarrass	enough
envelope	especially	exaggerate	excellence	familiar
fascinate	favorite	finally	fourth	friend

Circle ten of these words that give you the most trouble. On another piece of paper, write each of the circled words five times each. Then write ten sentences using the ten words you did not circle.

fourth

eighth

ACTIVITY 149 Spelling List G–K

Name:_____

Date:_____

There are many words that are commonly misspelled by people of all ages. If you can memorize these, you will find yourself ahead of most fifth- and sixth-graders and even many adults. Here are 20 words that begin with the letters *G*, *H*, *I*, *J*, and *K*.

heroes	guarantee	humorous	immediately
instead	independence	knowledge	jealous
hospital	happiness	government	grateful
innocent	height	intelligence	governor
interest	judgment	interrupt	grammar

1. On another piece of paper, copy these words in alphabetical order.

2. On another piece of paper, write just five sentences using as many of these 20 words as possible.

ACTIVITY 150 Spelling List L–P

Name:_____

Date:_____

There are many words that are commonly misspelled by people of all ages. If you can memorize these, you will find yourself ahead of most fifth- and sixth-graders and even many adults. Here are 20 words that begin with the letters *L*, *M*, *N*, *O*, and *P*.

leisure	lightning	lying	millionaire	mischievous
necessary	noticeable	nuisance	occasion	occurred
opportunity	opposite	pamphlet	particular	permanent
pneumonia	possession	preferred	privilege	psychology

On another piece of paper, copy the words above into these three columns:

A) Words with tricky vowels   B) Words with tricky consonants   C) Words with tricky vowels and consonants

For group A, copy the words again, leaving out the vowels. Can you replace the vowels correctly without looking at the word list? Do the same thing with group B, leaving out the consonants. Then ask a friend to quiz you a few times on the words in group C.

ACTIVITY 151 Spelling List Q–S

Name: _____

Date: _____

There are many words that are commonly misspelled by people of all ages. If you can memorize these, you will find yourself ahead of most fifth- and sixth-graders and even many adults. Here are 20 words that begin with the letters *Q*, *R*, and *S*.

scissors	reference	surprise	rhythm
restaurant	straight	studying	superintendent
suspense	separation	quantity	recommend
receipt	safety	ridiculous	schedule
strengthen	sugar	similar	success

1. Write the words in alphabetical order on another piece of paper.
2. Choose four words with base words you can use to form more words. Write the word from this list, plus one or two more words with the same base.

   Example: safety ⟶ safely, safer

ACTIVITY 152 Spelling List T–Z

Name: _____

Date: _____

There are many words that are commonly misspelled by people of all ages. If you can memorize these, you will find yourself ahead of most fifth- and sixth-graders and even many adults. Here are 20 words that begin with the letters *T*, *U*, *V*, *W*, *X*, *Y*, and *Z*.

themselves	therefore	thief	thorough	thought
tomorrow	truly	unique	until	unusual
usually	vaccinate	vacuum	vegetable	villain
Wednesday	weight	weird	written	yacht

Circle ten of these words that give you the most trouble. On another piece of paper, write each of the circled words five times each. Then write ten sentences using the ten words you did not circle.

ACTIVITY 153 Editing to Correct a Variety of Spelling Errors

Name:_____

Date:_____

Circle evry mispelled or misused word you find in this activty.

1. What happened to commen sence?

2. It seams like nobody has it anymore!

3. For instance, a freind of mine sits the air conditioning at 65° F, and than she complanes that its too cold in the room!

4. Also, my Aunt shops from 9 A.M. untill 6 P.M. and then wonders why she dosen't feel like going out for diner.

5. Do knot let me forget to mention my nieghbor, Rick, who buys boxes of dog bisciuts every week and then grumbles to the cashier about the high price of his groceries!

6. As I said, wear's all the inteligence?

How many words did you circle? _____ We found an even 20!

ACTIVITY 154 Editing to Correct a Variety of Errors

Name:_____

Date:_____

Rewrite each sentence, making sure to correct all the errors in spelling, capitalization, and the use of apostrophes.

1. Its amazeing how many poeple today still don't use the Internet

   _____

2. but it dosen't phase my grandma richmond at all.

   _____

3. she clicks around from here to their, shoping, chating, and researching, to.

   _____

4. My grandmother now has a laptop that she takes on cite-seeing drives.

   _____

5. Somtims she let's grandpa use it to play a game while shes driveing.

   _____

ACTIVITY 155 Editing to Correct a Variety of Errors

Name:_____

Date:_____

One portion of each sentence contains an error. Write the letter of that section in the blank. Then rewrite the sentence correctly on the line below.

	A	B	C	
1.	Its going	to take a long time	to reach California.	_____
2.	At this rate,	we'll not get their	this week.	_____
3.	It's posible	that we won't make it	this month, either.	_____
4.	I guess	it's to long of a trip	from Michigan	_____
5.	Could you	just relax	and quite bugging me?	_____
6.	I am pedalling	this tricycle	as quickly as I can!	_____

ACTIVITY 156 Editing to Correct a Variety of Errors

Name:_____

Date:_____

On another piece of paper, rewrite this paragraph correcting mistakes in spelling, capitalization, and use of apostrophes.

The restarant manager decided to hold a traning night for his new employees. He called in the new waiters, waitress, and chiefs. He emphasized the importence of the customer.

"This is not about you," he began. "It's about them. without the customer, we wood have no restaurant, and you would have no job. Always remeber that."

Later a trainee asked a questoin. "Sir," he began, "if it's not about us, then how will these people get there food?"

After some very loud giggles, The manager resumed his speech.

"okay, so it's about all of us. Let's just agree that they get they're food frist."

ACTIVITY 157   Alphabetical Order: 1st and 2nd letter

Name:_____

Date:_____

1.	_10_ yam	_____may_____	_4_
2.	____ tub	_____	____
3.	____ stab	_____	____
4.	____ rats	_____	____
5.	____ reward	_____	____
6.	____ peels	_____	____
7.	____ top	_____	____
8.	____ slap	_____	____
9.	____ ten	_____	____
10.	____ parts	_____	____

A. First, number the words on the left in alphabetical order, from 1 to 10.

B. Then, in the middle blank, rewrite each word from back to front.

C. Finally, number the new words in alphabetical order from 1 to 10 in the blanks on the right.

The first one has been done for you.

ACTIVITY 158   Alphabetical Order: 1st, 2nd, and 3rd letters

Name:_____

Date:_____

Here are 12 titles from a book of children's songs. Put the song titles in alphabetical order by their first word, unless the first word is *The*. *The* is not included when alphabetizing titles.

1. ____ *The Bear Went Over the Mountain*

2. ____ *Do Your Ears Hang Low?*

3. ____ *The Wheels on the Bus*

4. ____ *The Name Game*

5. ____ *Eency Weency Spider*

6. ____ *Monkeys Jumping on the Bed*

7. ____ *The Elephant*

8. ____ *B-I-N-G-O*

9. ____ *Clementine*

10. ____ *Twinkle, Twinkle*

11. ____ *The Hokey Pokey*

12. ____ *The Barnyard Song*

On another piece of paper, make your own list of ten song titles. Number them in alphabetical order. Or, trade lists with a friend and number each other's list.

ACTIVITY 159 Alphabetical Order: 3rd and 4th letter

Name:_____

Date:_____

Sometimes two words have the same letters at the beginning, but one word is shorter than the other. When alphabetizing these words, the shorter word is listed first.
Example: Can is listed before *candy* in the dictionary.

Which name comes first in alphabetical order? Circle your choice.

1. Anna, Anne, Ann

2. Joe, Joshua, John

3. Sarah, Sara, Serene

4. Allison, Alice, Alli

5. Steven, Steve, Stephen

6. Lucas, Luke, Lyle

7. Cole, Cody, Connor

8. Kate, Katy, Katelyn

9. Micah, Mike, Michael

10. Matthew, Matt, Mathias

11. Brianca, Britannia, Brock

12. Don, Douglas, Doug

Anna Smith   - 223-7985
Sarah Smith - 222-5487
Cole Smive   - 222-6325
Mike Snock   - 223-4185
Brianca Snope - 223-9824
Joe Sopher   - 223-8426
Lucas Soster - 222-7035
Allison Sotten - 222-2258
Luke Sprinkle - 228-0568

ACTIVITY 160 Alphabetical Order

Name:_____

Date:_____

Can you think of a word that comes between each pair below? In the blank, write a word of your choice that comes between the two words alphabetically.
Example: tonight   *tooth*   topsoil

1. notebook _____ nourish

2. noun _____ nowhere

3. numeral _____ nutcracker

4. oath _____ oblong

5. okra _____ omelet

6. open _____ oppose

7. pack _____ page

8. pajamas _____ panel

9. party _____ passing

10. pecan _____ peek

11. punish _____ purple

12. quill _____ quotient

13. rabbit _____ radar

14. rash _____ ravel

ACTIVITY 161 **Alphabetical Order**

Name: _____

Date: _____

Write the names of these 14 *B* countries in alphabetical order on the lines below.

Botswana	Bhutan	Bangladesh	Belguim	Bolivia
Belize	Burundi	Bahrain	Belarus	Barbados
Benin	Bahamas	Bulgaria	Brazil	

1. _____
2. _____
3. _____
4. _____
5. _____
6. _____
7. _____
8. _____
9. _____
10. _____
11. _____
12. _____
13. _____
14. _____

How many of these can you find on a world map or globe?

ACTIVITY 162 **Alphabetical Order**

Name: _____

Date: _____

Think hard for this one! What's the nearest word you can name that comes immediately before and immediately after each word given here? Write your best answers in the blanks.

Example: _____*sleep*_____ sleet _____*sleeve*_____

1. _____ jam _____
2. _____ petal _____
3. _____ tumble _____
4. _____ vinyl _____
5. _____ woman _____
6. _____ alive _____
7. _____ drop _____
8. _____ furnace _____
9. _____ guest _____
10. _____ mover _____

Now check your classroom dictionary.

Did you get the closest words possible?

ACTIVITY 163 Using Guide Words

Name:_____

Date:_____

Decide if the words in the list belong on the *rhubarb – right* dictionary page or the *rim – robber* page. Then write the words for each page in alphabetical order.

 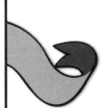

A. rhubarb – right	**B. rim – robber**
1. _____	1. _____
2. _____	2. _____
3. _____	3. _____
4. _____	4. _____
5. _____	5. _____
6. _____	6. _____

roast
ribbon
rhyme
rich
risky
ridge
ring
risen
ride
ripple
riot
rifle

ACTIVITY 164 Using Guide Words

Name:_____

Date:_____

On each page, you will find two guide words. Tell if the words listed under them are on that page, before that page, or after that page. An example is done for you.

O = on that page   **B** = before that page   **A** = after that page

dancer – data	**eerie – eighteen**	**finch – fire**
1. daisy _B_	5. egg _____	9. fir _____
2. date _____	6. edit _____	10. find _____
3. daring _____	7. eight _____	11. finally _____
4. dangle _____	8. eighty _____	12. finger _____

hitch – hold	**llama – locate**	**ostrich – our**
13. hit _____	17. loafer _____	21. other _____
14. hole _____	18. lock _____	22. ours _____
15. hollow _____	19. lizard _____	23. oriole _____
16. hog _____	20. lobby _____	24. orphan _____

Answers Keys

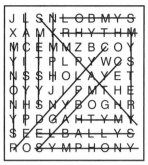

Activity 1 (p. 1)
1. shrimp   2. scratch
3. shrieks, screams   4. shreds
5. shrunk   6. shrug   7. scraped
Sentences will vary.

Activity 2 (p. 1)
1. strike, street, strong, string, stripe,
   straight, strange, streak
2. squid, squirm, squeeze, squint,
   square, squeak
3. When your nose is squashed
   against the ceiling!

Activity 3 (p. 2)
1. Answers will vary.
2. *Sc* is followed by *a* or *o. Sk* is
   followed by *a, i, u, o,* or *y.*

Activity 4 (p. 2)
1. school   2. scissors   3. scheme
4. science 5. schooner   6. scene
7. scientist 8. scholar   9. scenery
10. scepter   Sentences will vary.

Activity 5 (p. 3)
A. pheasant, phlox, phoebe (bird),
   nephew, physician, elephant,
   pharmacist
B. phonics, alphabet, hyphen
C. physician, nephew, pharmacist

Activity 6 (p. 3)
1. wrench   2. wring   3. wrist
4. wrestlers 5. wreck   6. wrath
7. wrapper   8. wrinkle
Definitions will vary.

Activity 7 (p. 4)
1. question   2. mention 3. attention
4. suggestion 5. essential 6. potential
7. exhaustion 8. invention

Activity 8 (p. 4)
Answers will vary.

Activity 9 (p. 5)
Possible answers include:
1. facts 2. length   3. guesses
4. aunt   5. effort, lettuce
6. cattle, grass   7. spend, tent

Activity 10 (p. 5)
Possible answers include:
1. bread, lead, dread
2. treasure, pleasure, measure
3. weather, feather, leather
4. breath, death   5. lead, read, said
Sentences will vary.

Activity 11 (p. 6)
Circled letters are underlined:
1. visitor   2. finishing 3. dictionary
4. minimum 5. inquire   6. inside
7. primitive

Activity 12 (p. 6)
1. myth   2. rhythm   3. symbol
4. cymbals 5. nymph   6. symphony
7. system   8. syllable   9. cylinder
10. physical 11. mystery 12. sympathy
13. synonym   Bonus Word: gyp

Activity 13 (p. 7)
1. follow   2. common or cotton
3. dollar   4. gobble or goggle
5. robber or roller 6. broccoli
7. waffle   8. gossip   9. nozzle
10. shopper 11. swallow 12. throttle
Sentences will vary.

Activity 14 (p. 7)
Answers will vary.

Activity 15 (p. 8)
1. fine   2. plan   3. theme   4. rode
5. quit   Sentences will vary.

Activity 16 (p. 8)
Circled words are in bold:
    The plan for the Robins to win the
baseball **game** was **plain** to everyone.
The way to make the Eagles strike out
was for the Robins to wave their arms,
race around the dugout, and scream
loudly enough to give every Eagle
player a **headache**.
    It was now the **eighth** inning and
time to work the plan. The score was
tied. The coach was **afraid** his **team**
might not pull through.
    "I **aim** to win this game!" Coach
yelled. "Let's **claim** victory! Let's **shape**
up! Let's wave our arms and scream!"
The coach had already **strained** his
voice enough. "No **complaining**, team.
Just pay close attention. Hit. Run.
Throw. Catch. And make the other
team strike out. It's very simple."
    The pep talk **paid** off. The Robins
struck out all the batters in the **eighth**
and ninth innings. And the last Robins
batter hit a home run way out of the
park!

Activity 17 (p. 9)
1. scheme 2. complete   3. disease
4. frequent 5. immediate *6. seaweed
7. seek   8. zebra   *9. leave
*10. beat   Pairs will vary.

Activity 18 (p. 9)
1. buy*, boy, soy, sly*, fly*, fry*, dry*,
   try*, cry*
2. dill, pill, pile*, mile*, mild*, mind*,
   find*, fine*, dine* Puzzles may vary.

Activity 19 (p. 10)
Teacher check lines over long *o.*
Open: radio, broken, ocean, local, hotel
Closed: clothing, postage, toaster,
        golden, hostess

Activity 20 (p. 10)
1. barbecue 2. amuse   3. rescue
4. future   5. humor   6. usual
7. statue, huge   8. pursue

Activity 21 (p. 11)
1. t   2. c   3. e   4. f   5. r   6. e
7. p   PERFECT   Words will vary.

Activity 22 (p. 11)
1. dunes   2. tuba, flute   3. rule
4. salute   Sentences will vary.

Activity 23 (p. 12)
1. straw   2. strong   3. daughter
4. awful   5. applaud   6. August
7. audience 8. coffee   9. claw
10. awkward   Sentences will vary.

Activity 24 (p. 12)
Possible answers include:
1. garden, garbage, garlic
2. charcoal, charter, charming
3. marker, market, marble
4. target, tardy, tartar
5. startle, starboard, starfish
6. barber, bargain, barbell
7. warden, warranty, warbler
Sentences will vary.

Activity 25 (p. 13)
Possible answers include:
3-letter: ore, for
4-letter: oral, form, odor
5-letter: order, forge, flora, minor
6-letter: ordeal, corner, floral, reform,
        flavor

Activity 26 (p. 13)
Correct words:
perfect, alert, curtain, adverb, return,
observe, survey, transfer, person

Activity 27 (p. 14)
1. towel   2. nickel   3. level
4. signal   5. mental   6. cancel
7. vocal   8. loyal   9. sandals
10. plural   11. model   12. pedal

Activity 28 (p. 14)
1. create 2. ruin   3. quiet
4. eon   5. triangle 6. audio 7. trial

Activity 29 (p. 15)
1. believe, thief, chief, piece, lie, brief,
   yield
2. ceiling, receive, deceive
3. eighty, freight, vein, weight

Activity 30 (p. 15)
Sentences will vary.

Activity 31 (p. 16)
1. friend, niece, retrieve, grief
2. perceive, receipt, conceited
3. sleigh, beige
4. neither, their, weird, ancient, protein

83

Activity 32 (p. 16)
1. U   2. S   3. E   4. A   5. D   6. I
7. C   8. T   9. I   10. O   11. N   12. A
13. R   14. Y   USE A DICTONARY

Activity 33-36 (p. 17-18)
Answers will vary.

Activity 37 (p. 19)
1. niece   2. Neither   3. usually
4. field   5. ancient   6. weird
7. conceited

Activity 38 (p. 19)
Corrected words are in bold:

I can't **believe** I helped to catch a real **thief**, right in our own **neighborhood**! It started when I left the dog kennel outside by mistake. Inside was a doggy **protein** treat. The door was propped open with a stick. I'd taken Doggy outside for a **brief** run, but then I'd walked him back inside the house and forgot about the kennel. (I am **usually** not that forgetful.)

I went to bed promptly at **eight** minutes after ten. (I always listen to the weather forecast on the nightly news before turning in. And since my little brother and I sleep in **separate** rooms, I can stay up later than he can.) At ten twenty-eight, while I was still staring up at the **ceiling**, there was a whang-bang-snap sound in the backyard. I jolted up in my bed and raced outside. Trapped inside the dog kennel was a gigantic raccoon! Immediately, I was joined by Mr. Pibbles from next door.

"Congratulations, **friend**! You caught the nighttime bandit who is **probably** responsible for stealing at least five of Martha's homemade boysenberry pies." (I wondered why anyone, or anything, would want any of those.) "I'm happy to give you the reward we've been offering," Mr. Pibbles exclaimed most enthusiastically.

"What's the reward?" I asked.

"It's a dozen boysenberry pies! I'll **retrieve** a **piece** for you right now. We'll bake the rest for you **tomorrow**," he replied.

This may sound **weird**, but I don't think I'll forget and leave the kennel outside ever again.

Activity 39 (p. 20)
1. than, than 2. then   3. then
4. than   5. then, then 6. than

Activity 40 (p. 20)
Answers will vary.

Activity 41 (p. 21)
1. already   2. all ready   3. already
4. all ready 5. all ready, already
6. already, all ready

Activity 42 (p. 21)
1. Right 2. Right 3. Wrong 4. Wrong
5. Right 6. Right 7. Right

Activity 43 (p. 22)
1. any one   2. everyday 3. anyone
4. every day 5. anyone

Activity 44 (p. 22)
1. dessert 2. Desert, a
3. desert, a; desert, b   4. desert, b
5. desert, b; dessert   6. desert, a

Activity 45 (p. 23)
Answers will vary.

Activity 46 (p. 23)
1. loose   2. loose   3. lose   4. loses
5. loosely 6. lose   7. lose

Activity 47 (p. 24)
1. accept, except   2. accept
3. except   4. Except   5. accept
6. accept, except

Activity 48 (p. 24)
1. sit, set   2. lay, set   3. lie
4. set, lie   5. sit

Activity 49 (p. 25)
1. through   2. thorough 3. through
4. thorough 5. through 6. through
7. thorough

Activity 50 (p. 25)
Answers will vary.

Activity 51 (p. 26)
1. quiet   2. than   3. quite
4. altogether or quite   5. then
6. all together   7. already

Activity 52 (p. 26)
1. really, dessert 2. every day, Anyone
3. quite 4. dessert, breathe 5. lose
6. Sometimes, sit 7. Then   8. Already

Activity 53 (p. 27)

Let me tell you about our sixth-grade field trip. It was **quite** a trip! First, everyone loaded on the bus at six a.m. **Then** we drove for two hours. Everyone wondered if the trip would be worth the drive. By the end of the day, we were **altogether** certain it was!

We met Governor Fisher. We met all the members of his cabinet, **except** for the secretary of state. We had to **sit** very **quietly** during some important meetings. We dined in the governor's mansion. These are not **everyday** activities for us!

When we climbed back on the bus, the teachers asked if we were **all ready** for one more stop. The bus driver winked, and the next thing we knew we were at Frosty's Ice Cream Parlor. Every one of us graciously **accepted** a free ice cream cone, compliments of the governor!

Activity 54 (p. 27)

The **chief** of police was puzzled. **Every day** for a week now, a mysterious caller phoned him with the same message:

"**Sit** down at noon, Chief. We're coming to see you!" What was he to think? He didn't **usually receive** such strange calls.

He asked his fellow officers to **weigh** in on the subject. What would they do? The results were mixed.

Finally, on Thursday night, the chief reached his decision. "The voice sounds muffled but friendly. I'll **probably** regret this, but **tomorrow** I will be **all ready**. I'll be **sitting** at my desk at noon. But my deputies will also stand ready if anything **weird** should happen.

Friday at noon, there was a knock on his door. "Surprise!" yelled his grandkids **all together**. "We thought we'd never get you here at the right time. We've been waiting all week to give you a surprise birthday party!"

The chief took a deep **breath**. If he hadn't been at his desk at noon today, he would have had a bad **conscience** for a very long time.

Activity 55 (p. 28)
1. to   2. too, to   3. two   4. to, too
5. to   6. to, too   7. two

Activity 56 (p. 28)

It didn't take Nick **too** long to learn how **to** use the computer. At the very young age of **two**, he crawled up on his mom's desk chair and found the power switch. He clicked on the mouse and in **two** seconds, he was playing a fast-paced game and reading an online encyclopedia. Nick's mother walked into the room. She was **too** astonished to speak.

When he was three, Nick's mom was writing a book called, *How to Parent a Genius*. Nick tried not to be **too** picky, but he circled all her spelling mistakes!

Activity 57 (p. 29)
1. there   2. there 3. their
4. Their, they're   5. they're, their
6. their   7. their

Activity 58 (p. 29)
Answers will vary.

Activity 59 (p. 30)
1. threw   2. through   3. through
4. through 5. threw, through
6. through

Activity 60 (p. 30)
1. brake   2. break   3. break   4. break
5. break   6. break   7. brakes

Activity 61 (p. 31)
1. bored, board   2. creak
3. soar, creek   4. feat
5. sores, feet, heels, heal
6. main   7. mane

Activity 62 (p. 31)
1. colonel
2. coup
3. chute
4. choral
5. draught
6. martial
7. sighed
8. pier
9. towed
10. rapt   11. flair   12. yoke
13. wee   14. faze   15. doe
Sentences will vary.

Activity 63 (p. 32)
1. guessed/guest   2. fur/fir
3. bale/bail   4. site/sight   5. vein/vain
6. rein/reign 7. lone/loan
Bonus: cite, vane, rain

Activity 64 (p. 32)
2. lien   3. berth   4. bawl   5. suite
Sentences will vary.

Activity 65 (p. 33)
1. seed, cede   2. wholly, holy
3. knew, gnu, new   4. soared, sword
5. throne, thrown   6. flocks, phlox
7. seller, cellar   8. urn, earn
9. ewe, you, yew   10. write, rite, right
11. toad, towed   12. serial, cereal
Sentences will vary.

Activity 66 (p. 33)
1. capital, 3 2. Capitol, 4 3. capital, 2
4. capital, 1 5. capitol, 5

Activity 67 (p. 34)
1. principle, 5   2. principal, 1
3. principal, 2   4. principle, 6
5. principal, 4   6. principal, 3

Activity 68 (p. 34)
1. stationary, 2 2. stationery, 4
3. stationary, 1 4. stationary, 3
Sentences will vary.

Activity 69 (p. 35)
You **would not** believe this
unless it happened **to you**! I was
sitting **by** myself, **close** to a tree. I
planned to **read** a book. **But** suddenly,
some pointy thing poked me in my
shoulders. I jumped up in fright. I was
too scared to look behind me to **see**
what it was. But finally, I did. It was
two giant **moose**, with big antlers and
everything! I didn't **know** I was near
their home. **You** probably think I'm a

liar, but it really happened to me. **So** it
could happen to you, **too**! Beware…
Bonus: **Peace** should be **piece**.

Activity 70 (p. 35)
We took a tour through the nation's
Capitol. It was **sweet** to see where
Congress meets to **write** laws. To see
the **principles** of democracy in action
was awesome. We were **wholly** in awe
through the entire tour. We watched a
debate in the House. **There** was a **real**
difference of opinion on a new **tax**. One
person was so **tied** to his opinion that
you would have had to move him off
the floor with a bulldozer!

Activity 71 (p. 36)
1. he'd   2. she's   3. you're 4. I'm
5. there'd 6. won't   7. who's
8. they're 9. doesn't 10. mustn't
11. there'd 12. she'll 13. there had,
                              there would

Activity 72 (p. 36)
1. Who's   2. That's   3. I've
4. You've   5. doesn't   6. You're
7. It's   8. weren't, wouldn't

Activity 73 (p. 37)
Possible answers include:
1. We couldn't get any sleep last night.
2. Mrs. Axe's cat wouldn't stop howling.
3. That was no way to spend the night.
4. Mrs. Axe says there's nothing to be
   done.
5. My dad says there's no truth to that.
6. He bought us all earplugs that
   won't let any sound through.

Activity 74 (p. 37)
Correct these statements:
1. It's about time…
2. … until they're in small…
5. … pulp away from its skin.
6. When you're all done…
8. If it's not too hot…

Activity 75 (p. 38)
Possible answers include:
1. semiannual, hemisphere
2. bicycle, biceps
3. octopus, octet
4. century, centimeter
5. tricycle, triplets
6. quadrilateral, quadruple
7. multilateral, multifunctional

Activity 76 (p. 38)
1. uncover   2. disconnect 3. illogical
4. irresponsible 5. discomfort
6. impossible   7. irregular
8. unbelievable 9. inability 10. illegal
11. impatient   12. inexpensive

Activity 77 (p. 39)
1. c   2. a   3. b   4. f   5. d
6. g   7. e   Added words will vary.

Activity 78 (p. 39)
1. supervise   2. correspond
3. prologue   4. paramedic
5. pro-labor   6. synchronize
7. prearrange   8. synchronize,
                        correspond

Activity 79 (p. 40)
Answers include:
pregame, pretest, postgame, posttest,
transform, transport, subway

Activity 80 (p. 40)
1. dissatisfied   2. unnamed
3. misshapen   4. unneeded
5. disregard   6. repay
7. autobiography

Activity 81 (p. 41)
1. stopping   2. laughable
3. controlled 4. beginning 5. sleeting
6. knotting   7. planned
8. regretted 9. quitting 10. sleeping

Activity 82 (p. 41)
1. satisfying 2. busier   3. emptying
4. worrying   5. qualifying 6. crying
7. greedily   8. staying   9. hungrily
10. marrying 11. mysterious

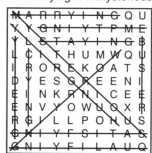

Activity 83 (p. 42)
1. correct   2. correct   3. creatively
4. writing   5. correct   6. lifeless
7. polluting   8. correct   9. correct
10. correct 11. imagining 12. correct

Activity 84 (p. 42)
1. arranged, arrangement
2. believed, believing
3. caring, careless
4. safely, safety
5. forgiveness, forgiving
6. namely, naming

Activity 85 (p. 43)
1. truly   2. wisdom   3. possibly
4. width   5. argument 6. terribly
7. wholly   8. judgment 9. awful
10. manageable 11. canoeing
12. mileage

Activity 86 (p. 43)
1. loudly   2. noisily   3. reliably
4. thoughtfully 5. accusingly
6. decisively   7. wisely

Activity 87 (p. 44)
Answers will vary.

Activity 88 (p. 44)
1. heaviness   2. darkness
3. helpless   4. careless, penniless
5. likeness   6. sleepless
7. goodness'

Activity 89 (p. 45)
1. laughable, c   2. believable, f
3. visible, a   4. collectible, g
5. payable, e   6. removable, b
7. manageable, d

Activity 90 (p. 45)
1. occupation   2. suggestion
3. punctuation   4. television
5. explanation, division
6. examination, decision

Activity 91 (p. 46)
1. assistant   2. president   3. informant
4. immigrant   5. accountant   6. resident
Sentences will vary.

Activity 92 (p. 46)
1. e   2. a   3. e   4. e   5. e
6. a   7. a   8. a   9. a   10. e
11. a   12. e   13. e   14. a   15. a
Sentences will vary.

Activity 93 (p. 47)
Possible words: illegal, illegally, legally,
unchangeable, changeable, misdirect,
misdirection, direction, helpful,
unhelpful, unimaginable, imaginable,
disappearance, disappear, preferable,
preferably. Sentences will vary.

Activity 94 (p. 47)
spelling, Possibly, dissatisfied,
discussion, disappearance,
reasonable, rewritten
Variations may be possible.

Activity 95 (p. 48)
1. Yes   2. Yes   3. No   4. Yes
5. No   6. Yes   7. Yes   8. Yes
9. No   10. No   11. Yes   12. Yes
13. Yes   14. No
Teacher check the words that make up
the compounds.

Activity 96 (p. 48)
1. afternoon   2. eavesdrop
3. lunchtime   4. spaceship
5. breakfast   6. evergreen
7. warehouse   8. woodchuck
Sentences will vary.

Activity 97 (p. 49)
Possible answers include:
1. shortbread, gingerbread, cornbread
2. brainstorm, thunderstorm,
   snowstorm
3. taillight, headlight, lamplight,
   firelight, moonlight
4. nighttime, daytime, anytime,
   everytime
5. bookworm, hookworm, tapeworm
6. flagstone, limestone, headstone,
   whetstone

Activity 98 (p. 49)
1. lifeguard   2. wastebasket
3. driveway   4. gentleman
5. baseball   6. timeline
7. somewhere

Activity 99 (p. 50)
Possible words include: clockwork,
football, timekeeper, snowman,
stopwatch, airfare, cartwheel,
classroom, cottontail, forewarn,
lamppost, moonlight, rattlesnake,
sidewalk.

Activity 100 (p. 50)
A. flashlight, grandfather, babysitter,
   fireworks, southwest
B. high school, booby trap, seat belt
C. miles-per-hour, half-truth, self-serve,
   great-grandchild, editor-in-chief, ex-
   manager
Note: Not all dictionaries agree on
the division of some words. Accept
answers that your students may find in
their classroom dictionaries.

Activity 101 (p. 51)
Answers will vary.

Activity 102 (p. 51)
1. re - done, B   2. suit - case, A
3. shore - line, A   4. co - pay, B
5. back - yard, A   6. eye - brow, A
7. re - write, B   8. bi - ceps, B
9. house - work, A   10. birth - day, A
11. dis - arm, B   12. soft - ware, A

Activity 103 (p. 52)
1. wis - dom   2. com - posed
3. writ - ten   4. swim - ming
5. as - sure   6. cam - pers
7. af - ford   8. un - safe
9. hap - pen   10. set - tle
11. dis - putes   12. jus - tice

Activity 104 (p. 52)
IN THE COUGH-A-TERIA

Activity 105 (p. 53)
jack - et
jack - pot
jag - uar
jas - mine
jay - walk
jeal - ous
jew - el
jok - er
jum - ble, junc - tion

Activity 106 (p. 53)
1. cre - a - tive   2. tour - ist
3. re - ac - tion   4. one syllable
5. nui - sance   6. brief - ly
7. he - ro - ic   8. auc - tion
9. one syllable   10. ma - te - ri - al
11. re - ceiv - a - ble   12. bu - reau

Activity 107 (p. 54)
1. 5   2. 6   3. 5   4. 5   5. 5
6. 5   7. 7   8. 4   9. 4   10. 4
11. 4   12. 4   Sentences will vary.

Activity 108 (p. 54)
1. am-a-teur   2. coun-ter-feit
3. dis-ap-pear   4. ex-pe-ri-ence
5. gov-ern-ment   6. his-to-ry
7. im-me-di-ate   8. leg-is-la-tion

Activity 109 (p. 55)
Across: 1. watches   5. gorillas
       6. buzzes   7. naps   8. steps
Down: 1. walruses   2. horizons
       3. pastures   4. elms   6. buses
(Busses is an acceptable plural for bus,
but it doesn't fit into the crossword.)

Activity 110 (p. 55)
1. dictionaries   2. stories   3. decoys
4. countries   5. bays   6. treaties
7. parties   8. alleys   9. trolleys
10. categories   11. worries   12. studies

Activity 111 (p. 56)
1. leaves, churches   2. OK   3. OK,
halves   4. OK   5. OK   6. themselves

Activity 112 (p. 56)
1. potatoes   2. ratios   3. radios
4. tomatoes   5. patios
6. Tornadoes or Tornados

Activity 113 (p. 57)
1. oxen   2. mice   3. feet   4. moose
5. corps   6. fungi   7. geese   8. teeth
9. crises   Bonus: octopuses

Activity 114 (p. 57)
    Three **geese** flew into a shopping
mall full of men, **women**, and **children**.
They squawked and honked. The
animals waddled through aisles of
shoes, **dresses**, and slacks. They
flapped by coats, scarves, gloves, and
mittens. Finally, they flew into a huge
tank full of fish and turtles, sending
splashes of water onto books, toys,
ferns, and **cactuses** (or **cacti**).
    Gasps could be heard throughout
the mall. "How could this have happened? Why were the doors all left
open? Why didn't some **guards** shoo
them back outside?"
    Finally, some wise **guys** supplied
the answers. "Well, folks, maybe the
geese just needed some new **clothes!**"

Activity 115 (p. 58)
1. sugar   2. beauty   3. anger   4. silver
5. nature   6. happiness   7. love
8. gravel   9. intelligence   10. chaos

Activity 116 (p. 58)
Correct plurals are: batches, buffalo
(also buffaloes or buffalos), dirt, flour,
groups, hitches, juries, libraries,
ponies, smudges, squares, sheep,
swine, wharves or wharfs, zoos.
Stories will vary.

Activity 117 (p. 59)
1. dentist's   2. tiger's   3. newspaper's
4. match's   5. laptop's   6. straw hut's
7. vegetable's   8. classroom's
9. zookeeper's   10. balloon's

Activity 118 (p. 59)
1. mattress's tag   2. Congress's duty
3. business's motto
4. Royal Highness's crown
5. wilderness's mountains
6. Janis's and Boris's children
7. Arkansas's tourist bureau

Activity 119 (p. 60)
2. secretaries' envelopes
3. mice's cheese
4. women's coats
5. workers' income
6. teeth's enamel

Activity 120 (p. 60)
1. yours   2. OK   3. ours   4. OK
5. problem's   6. geniuses   7. OK

Activity 121 (p. 61)
1. PP, S   2. P, PP   3. SP, P   4. PP, P
5. P, P, P   6. SP, S, P   7. SP, SP

Activity 122 (p. 61)
1. it's   2. sale's   3. theirs
4. buys, clothes   5. dollars', pairs
6. sweaters'   7. shirt's   8. shoes'

Activity 123 (p. 62)
1. boxes   2. box's   3. boxes'
4. journey's   5. journeys'   6. its
Sentences will vary.

Activity 124 (p. 62)
Your penmanship needs a lot of work. You need to remember to cross all your t's and dot all your i's. When you write z's, they should not look like 2's. Have you ever read Betsy Fisher's papers? Try to get your writing to look more like hers. All of the Fishers have great handwriting. In fact, all of the Fishers' handwriting exceeds most of the teachers' handwriting I have seen. The Fishers certainly write better than the doctors I know. If you work hard, better penmanship can definitely be yours!

Activity 125 (p. 63)
1. When I read Shel Silverstein's book, I thought…
2. The twins, Jenn and Joe, are going to…
3. My favorite play is…
4. The best place to go…
5. I would travel…
Completed sentences will vary.

Activity 126-127 (p. 63-64)
Answers will vary.

Activity 128 (p. 64)
Big holes all over Australia!

Activity 129 (p. 65)
1. Every Saturday I like to help my grandma.
2. Sara's dad has a conference with Principal Jones at noon today.
3. President Billings just resigned his position at the university.
4. Reverend Patrick Smith will give the address on Friday.
5. Uncle Joe, Aunt Jill, and Grandpa Dole all came to my birthday party.
6. The attorneys listened as Judge Parsons gave them instructions.
7. My great-grandfather was a senator from Rhode Island.

Activity 130 (p. 65)
4678 W. Elm Dr.
Sometown, AK
Nov. 3, 2007
Dear Sally,
 Thanks for inviting me to your house for Thanksgiving. Unfortunately, Mom and Dad said that we can't make the trip to Alaska this year. I always have fun hanging out with you and my other Alaskan cousins, but my parents said that'll have to wait. Instead of flying to Alaska, I guess we're going to swim to Tahiti for our turkey. Go figure!
Sincerely,
Ryan

Activity 131 (p. 66)
1. "Every time I come to your theater," the customer complained, "your popcorn stinks!"
2. "Today, it's too salty. Last week, it was cold," he continued. "Next week, I expect it will be burnt!"
3. The manager replied, "Sir, I can see we have a problem here, and I'd like to correct it."
4. "Nothing, and I mean nothing," the customer began, "can make up for the damages I've suffered. I had to watch an entire three-hour movie with popcorn that was too salty!"
5. "Do you think," the grumbling man continued, "that I'll just pretend everything's okay and keep coming back here week after week?"
6. "Perhaps this will help," offered the manager. "We'll give you a year's supply of rental movies at your nearest video store. That way, you can watch your movies at home!"

Activity 132 (p. 66)
 Dad says I need a haircut. (I guess when I couldn't see my **dinner** plate, Dad figured it was time to do **something**.) Anyway, I'm going to Ned's shop **tomorrow** morning. **It's** always an interesting **experience** when I go **there**. Once Ned was giving a haircut to King Omar of Omarzia. Another time, he was **shaving** off the beard of Doctor Doolittle. The last time I was there (I **believe** it was last April), Ned was **trimming** the hair on the back of a gorilla. I wonder what will happen **tomorrow**!

Activity 133 (p. 67)
1. Friday   2. Monday   3. Wednesday
4. Tuesday   5. Thursday   6. Sunday
7. Saturday

Activity 134 (p. 67)
1. October   2. March   3. September
4. February   5. May   6. January
7. June   8. July   9. November
10. December   11. April, August

Activity 135 (p. 68)
1. August   2. Monday   3. June
4. Tuesday   5. December   6. February
7. April   8. Thursday   9. Wednesday
10. January   11. November   12. March
13. Sunday   14. October   15. Saturday
16. Friday   17. September   18. July

Activity 136 (p. 68)
Answers will vary.

Activity 137 (p. 69)
A. 1. five   2. eight   3. twelve
 4. thirteen   5. fourteen   6. fifteen
 7. nineteen   8. twenty   9. thirty
 10. forty   11. sixty   12. hundred
B. 1. eight   2. fifteen   3. five
 4. forty   5. fourteen   6. hundred
 7. nineteen   8. sixty   9. thirteen
 10. thirty   11. twelve   12. twenty

Activity 138 (p. 69)
1. three thousand, sixty-seven
2. forty-two thousand, nine hundred eighteen
3. eight hundred thirty-one thousand, fifty-six
4. one million, five hundred seventy-two thousand, four hundred thirty-seven
5. one hundred sixty-seven thousand, eight hundred forty-five
6. ninety-nine thousand, ninety-nine

Activity 139 (p. 70)
1. FORTY + FIFTY = NINETY
2. SIXTY + TEN = SEVENTY
3. FOURTEEN + THREE = SEVENTEEN
4. TWENTY + TWENTY = FORTY

Activity 140 (p. 70)
1. third   2. fifth   3. seventh   4. ten
5. s, r, v, d   6. h, h
7. FIFTIETH

Activity 141 (p. 71)
1. Mr. McDonald, Sr. or the senior Mr. McDonald
2. Mr. McDonald, Jr.,; James McDonald, D.D.S.
3. Mrs. McDonald
4. Gen. McDonald
5. McDonald, Sr.,

Activity 142 (p. 71)
Answers will vary.

Activity 143 (p. 72)
1. St.   2. Ave.   3. Blvd.   4. Dr.
5. Ct.   6. Pkwy. 7. Ln.   8. Rd. 9. Tr.
10.–11. Answers will vary. 12. Any five
of the following: MN, WI, IA, IL, MO,
AR, TN, MS, LA, KY
Activity 144 (p. 72)
meter (m), centimeter (cm), gram (g),
kilogram (g), milligram (mg), liter (L),
kiloliter (kL), ounce (oz.), pound (lb.),
ton (T), inch (in.), foot (ft.), yard (yd.),
cup (c.), pint (pt.), quart (qt.), gallon
(gal.), acre (no abbreviation)

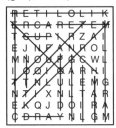

Activity 145 (p. 73)
1. 2: Mr. Smith works for the AFL-CIO.
2. 4: Frank White, D.D.S., used to play
   for the NFL.
3. 1: My aunt is the president of Think
   Tank, Inc.
4. 2: William S. Quinton hopes to work
   for the FBI.
5. 2: Pvt. Mark Brown is in the USMC.
Activity 146 (p. 73)
Dear Gene,
   This **morning** I heard back from
the **doctor**. My test results are all **okay**.
That's really good news. I'm sure I'll
save a lot of **money** if I don't have to go
back to see the **doctor** again!
   By the way, yesterday was great. It
was at least 70 **degrees** outside. Becca
and I flew our kites about 100 **feet**
before the lines snapped.
   Tomorrow I'm going to take Becca
to meet the **reverend**, and we'll set our
wedding date.
Sincerely,
Tom
Activity 147 (p. 74)
1. absence   2. accidentally
3. accommodate   4. achieve
5. acquaintance   6. amateur
7. appearance   8. attendance
9. beginning   10. believe
11. boundary   12. calendar
13. character   14. chocolate
15. column   16. committee
17. conscience   18. conscientious
19. continuous   20. convenience
Sentences will vary.
Activity 148 (p. 74)
Words and sentences will vary.

Activity 149 (p. 75)
1. government 2. governor 3. grammar
4. grateful 5. guarantee 6. happiness
7. height   8. heroes   9. hospital
10. humorous   11. immediately
12. independence 13. innocent
14. instead 15. intelligence 16. interest
17. interrupt18. jealous 19. judgment
20. knowledge Sentences will vary.
Activity 150 (p. 75)
Responses will vary.
Activity 151 (p. 76)
1. quantity 2. receipt 3. recommend
4. reference5. restaurant 6. rhythm
7. ridiculous8. safety   9. schedule
10. scissors 11. separation 12. similar
13. straight 14. strengthen
15. studying 16. success   17. sugar
18. superintendent 19. surprise
20. suspense
Activity 152 (p. 76)
Responses will vary.
Activity 153 (p. 77)
Circle **evry mispelled** or misused word
you find in this **actvity**.
1. What happened to **commen sence**?
2. It **seams** like nobody has it
   anymore!
3. For instance, a **freind** of mine **sits**
   the air conditioning at 65° F, and
   than she **complanes** that **its** too
   cold in the room!
4. Also, my **Aunt** shops from 9 A.M.
   untill 6 P.M. and then wonders why
   she **dosen't** feel like going out for
   diner.
5. Do **knot** let me forget to mention my
   nieghbor, Rick, who buys boxes of
   dog **bisciuts** every week and then
   grumbles to the cashier about the
   high price of his groceries!
6. As I said, **wear's** all the
   inteligence?
Activity 154 (p. 77)
1. **It's amazing** how many **people**
   today still don't use the Internet.
2. **But** it **doesn't faze** my **Grandma
   Richmond** at all.
3. **She** clicks around from here to
   there, shopping, chatting, and
   researching, **too.**
4. My grandmother now has a laptop
   that she takes on **sight**-seeing
   drives.
5. **Sometimes** she **lets Grandpa**
   use it to play a game while **she's
   driving**.
Activity 155 (p. 78)
1. A: It's going 2. B: we'll not get there
3. A: It's possible
4. B: it's too long of a trip

5. C: and quit bugging me?
6. A: I am pedaling
Activity 156 (p. 78)
   The **restaurant** manager decided
to hold a **training** night for **his** new
employees. He called in the new waiters,
waitresses, and **chefs**. He emphasized
the **importance** of the customer.
   "This is not about you," he began.
"It's about them. **Without** the customer,
we **would** have no restaurant, and you
would have no job. Always **remember**
that."
   Later a trainee asked a **question**.
"Sir," he began, "if it's not about us, then
how will these people get **their** food?"
   After some very loud giggles, **the**
manager resumed his speech.
   "**Okay**, so it's about all of us. Let's
just agree that they get **their** food **first**."
Activity 157 (p. 79)
2. 9, but, 2   3. 6, bats, 1   4. 3, star, 9
5. 4, drawer, 3   6. 2, sleep, 8
7. 8, pot, 7   8. 5, pals, 6 9. 7, net, 5
10. 1, strap, 10
Activity 158 (p. 79)
1. 2   2. 5   3. 12   4. 10   5. 6
6. 9   7. 7   8. 3   9. 4   10. 11
11. 8   12. 1
Activity 159 (p. 80)
1. Ann   2. Joe   3. Sara 4. Alice
5. Stephen 6. Lucas 7. Cody 8. Kate
9. Micah   10. Mathias 11. Brianca
12. Don
Activity 160 (p. 80)
Answers will vary.
Activity 161 (p. 81)
1. Bahamas   2. Bahrain
3. Bangladesh 4. Barbados
5. Belarus   6. Belguim 7. Belize
8. Benin   9. Bhutan 10. Bolivia
11. Botswana 12. Brazil   13. Bulgaria
14. Burundi
Activity 162 (p. 81)
Answers will vary. Consult a classroom
dictionary for the closest words.
Activity 163 (p. 82)
A. 1. rhyme 2. ribbon 3. rich   4. ride
   5. ridge 6. rifle
B. 1. ring   2. riot   3. ripple 4. risen
   5. risky   6. roast
Activity 164 (p. 82)
2. A   3. O   4. O   5. O   6. B
7. O   8. A   9. O   10. O   11. B
12. O 13. B   14. A 15. A   16. O
17. O 18. A   19. B 20. O   21. O
22. A 23. B   24. B